Crutches Tipped with Banana Peels

Laugh, Love, Heal

Crutches Tipped with Banana Peels

Laugh, Love, Heal

Joan Tenowich
Tom Tenowich

Humor Hill Publishing

Published in 2020 by Humor Hill Publishing

Facebook Page: Humor Hill Publishing

Email address: HumorHillPublishing@gmail.com

Cover design by Books Covered

ISBN 978-1-7349524-0-7

First Edition: August, 2020

With love to Linda,

who encouraged and guided us

Table of Contents

1   Rose Valley Falls 1

2   I'd Rather Be Surfing 11

3   Light Bulb Moment 17

4   Nursed through a Straw 21

5   My Third Ankle 29

6   My Friend Liz Vents. 31

7   Tom Mansplaining 33

8   Relationship on Ice 35

9   Pinpoint Accuracy 37

10   Doctor Five Potato to the Rescue 41

11   Job Retraining for Tom 47

12   Get It Together 53

13   My East Coast Cousin 57

14   My Daughter—My Parent 59

15   Caterpillar Crossing 61

16 They Also Serve Who Sit and Wait 63

17 Goodbye to Liz 67

18 Lisfranc Fusion Surgery 69

19 Morning Coffee at Noon 73

20 Caregiver / *Scaregiver* 77

21 Salmon or Salmonella .87

22 My Sixty-Second Bath .91

23 Casting 97

24 Saved by the Board 103

25 Emotional Lows and Highs 107

26 Visitors and Gifts 113

27 Casting Callback 117

28 Mortified 123

29 Physical Therapy—Round Two 129

30 Six-Month Checkup 135

31 One-Year Checkup 137

32 Coming Unscrewed 141

33 Takeaways 147

34 One More Step 149

35 Appendix A: Assemble Before Surgery 155

36 Appendix B: Insurance as a Second Language . .159

—   Acknowledgments 163

—   To Our Readers 165

CHAPTER ONE

Rose Valley Falls

Joan: Sculpted cliffs on either side cradled the canyon. Towering trees functioned as upside down brooms, cleaning the air instead of the ground. Our hike alongside wild roses and poppies gave no clue that our lives would soon abruptly change. The trail was leading toward a two-tiered, 300-foot waterfall, in Los Padres National Forest near Santa Barbara.

Tom: According to the latest Ranger hotline, a meandering climb on another trail would take us to a hillside covered with wildflowers. Bees and hikers were welcome.

Two chipmunks raced across in front of us, one chasing the other. Did the one in front steal a nut from the other's stash? Or was this a forest version of harassment? There's crime everywhere! It all seemed innocent since the perp was furry with cute stripes and a tail that shimmied.

Joan: Walking alongside ferns and shrubs, I soon felt peaceful. A canopy of oak and bay branches above, and the sun-dappled earth below, ringed me within the embrace of Mother Nature.

Tom: I waited patiently 'til the two women finished embracing, so we could move on.

Joan: Through gaps in the brush, we soon saw gushes of white water. The force of powerful rushing water from recent rainy seasons became apparent. Large rocks, originally parts of huge outcroppings, had gotten split off and swept downstream. They stood boldly alone— like little kids who had rushed ahead of their parents, then suddenly afraid they had gone too far, stopped to wait for them.

Tom: Rushing water had also pounded stones into sand. Gullies formed, where schools of tiny fish wriggled around aimlessly. They looked like those confused sperm in a Sex Ed video.

Joan: A tree trunk lay across the widening creek, offering balcony seating over the water below. The upended root ball revealed long, intertwined roots extending up and out in all directions like huge outstretched arthritic fingers. They once powerfully grasped the earth below, but could no longer hold their ground.

Tom and I got moving again, navigating the trail with its crisscrossing, rock-strewn streams. At about eye level on a few trees, flattish mushrooms grew in staggered layers. The multi-toned shapes were stacked much the way busboys pile dinner plates in a bin. These sculptural works of nature reminded me of artist Robert Therrien's seemingly precariously stacked dinner plates.

Tom: "Excuse me," I said, "did we just wander into a Mushroom Museum? I don't remember buying a ticket."

Joan: "Do you remember getting a marriage license? It covers things like this."

Tom: "Must have been in the fine print that guys don't read," I mumbled defensively. With Joan's art background, she sees art in surprising places. At the beach, I may remind her of the Statue of David. Okay, that's pushing it.

Shhh! Let's listen to the docent ...

Joan: Both the skewed wild mushrooms and Therrien's plates produced a paradox of balance. They seemed haphazard and

2

unsteady, but actually created counterbalances and visual excitement.

Tom: Interesting, Joan saw art images in wild mushrooms without ingesting them.The advantage of this kind of vision is that it will never need glasses.

For me, the forest was a place where stresses and responsibilities took a hike. It's always been more relaxing to go out for a dose of nature than to stay home and take a pill.

My favorite kind of hike has always been next to running water. It runs, I walk but we always arrive together. Perfect exercise! I never get tired.

Joan: The *ribbits* of frogs as they called for mates, and clusters of ladybugs often diverted my eyes from the trail. Raised tree roots had their *Gotcha* moment. My arms flapped and feet stumbled until I regained my balance. It was a fair trade-off for watching the locals in action.

Sounds of cascading water called out from behind massive boulders ahead. In a few moments, there it was—a majestic waterfall skimming downward over mossy petticoats. Falling water puffed *rainbowed* mist into the air. This scene was a show-stopper. It was the perfect place for lunch.

Tom settled nearby on a large rock and opened his backpack. That's where the water purifying straw, the bear bells, compass, whistle, the "thinner-than-a-deck-of-cards" emergency blanket, and other compact survival gear were nestled—along with our lunch.

Tom: Hey, I was prepared! That's why the salads I bought were resting on cold packs. I also brought a Swiss Army knife, but the only part I had been able to pull open was the tweezers. The Swiss Army must have the world's toughest fingernails.

Joan: More often than not, Tom had mini-eclairs or some other treat hidden in his pack. I always acted surprised!

Tom: Look, a guy knows when his wife's faking it. So I faked not knowing she's faking it. We're both phony, but it's fun.

Joan: Our forks passed in the air as we sampled each other's food. Everything tasted better in view of the falls. They were loud, so we ate and gazed more than talked. The rush of the water, however, was the ultimate white noise—soothing, meditative. Regardless, our picnic would soon turn to panic!

My eyes locked on a baby waterfall streaming over an alcove behind the main falls. As contrasting as they were, the macro and micro existed harmoniously. My telephoto lens was at home, so I needed to get closer with my iPhone.

Tom: I wasn't interested in seeing this micro in the macro, but asked Joan to get me a shot if a bear was taking a shower. She said bears prefer bubble baths, and off she went.

Joan: Tom stayed with our gear as I left and rounded a bend. Straight lines don't usually appear in nature, maybe encouraging us to meander, and appreciate the scenery. I did. I curved around another proud monolith, admiring its chiseled grottoes and bold prominences. Ahead I saw a little girl in a bright pink dress dancing on a huge flat-topped boulder. Watching *tickled pink's* delight up there made me smile. She took a few steps to the right, and obscured by trees, was out of my view.

As I walked farther, the happy little girl skipped by me holding her Dad's hand. They were the only people there, and they were leaving. Soon a six-foot high boulder confronted me. If I climbed on top of it as she must have, I'd be in perfect position to shoot the pint-sized waterfall. I jumped over a small stream running along the base of the boulder, and got a toehold a foot up its side. Grabbing onto the top of the boulder, I started pulling myself up. Thanks to the apes in my family tree, I made it!

The contrasting gentleness of the smaller bowed fall behind the roaring larger falls was enchanting. Crouched in position, I snagged several shots.

Tom: While Joan was feeding her photographic appetite, my mind drifted to flowering plants and bushes we had passed on the trail. Nobody had planted, fed or watered them. They just decided to grow there and put on a show. I marveled at what nature did on its own without a weekly gardener.

Joan: I couldn't wait to show Tom what I shot. I knew he'd be curious, despite what he said. When I stood up and turned to climb back down—*whoa*, what a surprise! Standing up there, the scene looked frightfully different. My eyes were now ten or eleven feet above the ground!

I suddenly realized my predicament. Getting down involved completely different logistics than climbing up. If I lowered myself hugging the boulder the way I came up, I could get a toe-hold on the same ledge. But like climbing down a ladder, in this case a boulder, I wouldn't be able to push away and jump backwards over the stream below. Only rabbits and ferrets can jump backwards, and they look pretty silly doing it.

I couldn't step down onto the same ledge with my body facing outward either. The narrow ledge that I had dug my toes into climbing up didn't extend out far enough to step down onto. *Bummer!* I looked around for a different way down. One side of the boulder was deep in water from the falls. Another dropped off steeply into tall shrubs, maybe housing unfriendly critters. Getting down from the far end of the boulder led to a steep, crude path that continued up to the higher waterfall. Tom would have no idea where I went.

The falls were noisy. Tom couldn't hear me calling him. Anxiety was building, plus I was embarrassed over the bind I had gotten into. I hated myself for even thinking this, but that little show-off in the pink dress made this all look too easy.

Tom: I wondered what was keeping Joan. How many pictures can you take of a tiny waterfall? If the water were flowing upwards, now that would be impressive! Of course, I've witnessed her more than once get enamored with a subject, like ancient tree trunks turned to stone in The Petrified Forest, or that red and blue lizard in Tanzania that looked like Spiderman. She wanted to snap them from different angles. Probably this time too. I was curious to see what she shot.

Joan: Boulders don't come with manuals, but I needed a plan. Jumping straight down into the water was the shortest distance. I rejected that because muddy shoes and pants wouldn't work with our planned dinner in picturesque Ojai (OH-hy).

Then I came up with a more daring choice. I would leap outward, over the stream bordering the boulder, and follow with a dirt landing right where I started. One minor concern, I needed to protect my right hip from any impact. It had been achy for a few months, but seemed to have recovered. I decided to land on my left foot, then follow immediately with my right for balance. Problem solved! I moved farther back on the boulder, focused, and with a running start, propelled myself out and over the water below. I was airborne longer than expected, like I was in slow-mo. *Uh-oh!* I must have jumped from higher than I thought. Finally I cleared the water by inches, and was about to touch down.

I lowered my left foot and *PFOOM!* I stuck my landing. Good job! In a nano second, a sharp pop under my arch shot around the inner side of my foot and finished on the top. With that I lost it—my balance, my footing and my cool. In one frightening and continuous action, I slammed down onto my left side, rolled onto my back and my legs flailed up in the air, expending the last of the downward/sideward/upward momentum! My right foot never got in on the action, never absorbed any impact. With such a careful plan, why did my body *turn turtle* like that?!

My left foot started throbbing. I got panicky and my fight or flight instinct kicked in. Suddenly I experienced an irrational desire to get away. How bizarre that my adrenaline-buzzed reaction was to run to safety. I tried, but two functioning feet were needed to do that. My body trembled. Feeling defeated, I slumped. Minutes went by. Then, *aha,* I knew exactly what to do! Make a *hiker down* call to 911. I pulled out my phone, you know, the one I always carry for emergencies. For this, my first true emergency, I was in a national forest out of cell range! Why couldn't Smokey have built a cell tower when he wasn't helping us prevent forest fires?! Irked and without options, I hollered to Tom again, but the big, noisy waterfall and the now dumb-ass baby waterfall still drowned out my calls.

Tom: I was getting concerned. I picked up all our stuff—Joan's backpack, a walking stick, two warm jackets that we didn't need, my backpack full of hiking supplies, plus empty food containers and bottles. There I was—part coatrack, part trash bin, part hiker and all husband—off to look for my shutterbug.

Joan: Never had I envisioned myself as an action figure. Did the spring greenery around me make me feel young enough to bend softly like new growth? Had jitteriness up on the boulder rattled my thinking into taking this leap? Or was it because I had seen the little girl up there alone, and later didn't, that I assumed she had jumped down herself? In retrospect, she had probably climbed up with her Dad's help, and her Dad had caught her coming down. I still don't know why I jumped, but this is a memoir not a mystery. I can't solve it for myself or for you.

Tom: The mystery for me became how this woman graduated eleventh in her high school class of 550 girls, and then won a scholarship to college. There must have been something they weren't teaching there, or maybe she was absent that day. No, that wouldn't explain it—she had perfect attendance. I did read a few years ago,

7

though, that her high school had closed. Finally something made sense.

Joan: Without other options, I painfully limped and lurched along the path, and turned toward where I had left Tom. I felt so relieved when I saw him coming! Seeing me limping badly—obviously I wasn't good at it—he dropped everything and ran to help me. He looked stunned as I leaned on him and told him what happened. I said I felt awful that I had ruined our day. "That's not important," he said, and gave me a hug.

Tom: I knew this was serious by the tears in Joan's eyes and how stiff her body felt. My arms sensed her tension and pain. She grimaced, dragging her left foot gingerly, as I helped her onto a nearby stump. She thought she had broken something. I asked if she wanted me to take off her shoe so she could check. She shook her head no. She said her foot would swell, and she might not be able to get her shoe back on.

Joan: Tom sat next to me with his arm around me. "It might be just a bad sprain cause they hurt a lot too," he said. He remembered reading that in the Sports section about injured players, so I tried to stay positive.

Tom: I knew Joan was in trouble when she readily sat down. This was a person who wouldn't give in to a 102 fever if there was work to be done. I feared she was hurt bad, just didn't know how bad. Frankly, I was scared too. How could I help her?

Joan: After some quiet moments together, we realized a more pressing concern—how would we get the half-mile back to our car?

Tom: As a husband I felt suddenly inadequate. Why couldn't I carry her to the car like Hugh Jackman or The Rock could have? If only I had worked out more. I should have joined a gym with a wife-lifting machine! A man's supposed to be strong. Construction workers are strong. Firemen are strong. Just Joan's luck, she married a writer. How strong do you have to be to push down little squares on a

8

keyboard? Okay, maybe strong emotionally since I faced empty pages every day. That made me feel better for half a second.

I wanted to help, but how? Then I got an idea. That's what writers do. I'd make a stretcher-like sled of tree branches and vines just like in western movies I'd seen. Joan then could lie down and I'd pull her. Of course, they hooked up their sleds to horses, but they were traveling much farther.

Nearby were a few young trees. I zeroed in on two branches, six to seven feet long, sturdy enough for the frame. They would saw off easily. Then I'd cut some vines and tie them to the frame in a crisscross pattern for Joan to lie on. I knew that somewhere in my backpack was a small saw. I dumped everything out and ran my hands through the pile. A saw was there all right—folded tight inside my Swiss Army knife! God help me! How long would it take to pick branches off with tweezers?!

Sadly my wife and I were left with each other and my walking stick. Joan leaned on my shoulder with one arm and on the stick with the other, slogging along the best she could.

Joan: Every muscle in my body tightened. Shooting pain caused me to stop often. About halfway back to the car, I noticed a squishy sensation accompanying each step on my injured foot, like I was walking in mud, *squoosh, squoosh.* Was my foot bleeding that much? I was afraid to check. I needed to stay focused on getting out of there.

Crossing a few streams on the way in was easy. But stepping on those same slippery rocks on the way out was a killer, even with my sherpa to lean on. I told Tom I couldn't go on. He said he understood, but that it would be a lonely drive home without me. We burst out laughing. Then he got a firm footing in the water, and lifted me over the most slippery and wobbly rocks. He kept encouraging me, saying it wasn't much farther. Yes, he was faking it again, but I knew, and he knew, that we had to keep going. Somehow, with three good feet between us, a few bad jokes, plus some TLC, I made it back to the trailhead.

My left shoe felt extremely tight as I angled myself into the car. Tom slid my seat back so I could raise my foot onto the dashboard. I took off my shoe and was relieved to see there was no blood on my sock. Like good soldiers, white blood cells had rushed to the scene to help. The swelling and additional fluid must have created that *squooshing* feeling. As we drove, the swelling outpaced any benefit from having my foot elevated. From the road, I called our Health Center. A doctor could see me, but by the time we drove back to LA, Radiology would be closed. I was told to ice my foot and come in the next morning.

When we got home, it hurt to step down, even lightly. Holding onto Tom, I hopped to the first doorstep and *butt-walked* up the few steps to our front door. Fortunately we live in a one-story house. I was able to hop to bed while Tom got me some ice.

Tom: I helped Joan gently remove her sock, and what greeted us was kinda like an eggplant with toes. Actually the purple was a two-inch band that wrapped around and under the middle of her foot. There was lots of other bruising on top. Gallows humor took over as Joan and I laughed that the rest of her foot looked more like a mix of pink grapefruit, a little rhubarb, the last banana from a big bunch and some pomegranates past their *Sell-by* date.

TIP #1: Wear hiking boots to hike. I wore athletic shoes that day because Rose Valley Falls was described as an easy hike. It was easy, but the additional support of my boots may have lessened my injury.

TIP #2: Stay on the hiking trail. Going off-trail increases the risk of accidents like mine, as well as exposure to poison ivy and other hazards. Snakes prefer to avoid us. Wandering off-trail into their turf will compel them to defend themselves.

CHAPTER TWO

I'd Rather Be Surfing

Joan: I was up early the next morning. Sleep had been driven off by pain. Tom rolled his office chair in to help me maneuver to the bathroom and kitchen, then to our car after breakfast. At our Health Center, Tom arranged for me to be wheeled from the parking lot to a table where X-rays were taken. My toes, foot and ankle hung morbidly like a deflating blimp. Then my kindly Primary Care doctor, Dr. One Potato, not his actual surname but the first in a sequence of doctors, came in smiling with comforting news that there were no fractures. I was given a referral and told to see a podiatrist for follow-up. The podiatrist was fully booked, but he would fit me in. A nurse adjusted my crutches and gave me a fifteen-second demo on how to use them.

Tom: Joan had never used crutches, but the brief instruction qualified as a crash course, so to speak. The office floor wasn't slippery. Joan's movements just made it look that way. I stayed close.

Joan: Luckily traffic on Pacific Coast Highway moved at a moderate weekday pace. The expanse of rippled sand, and surfers catching waves under California blue skies was a soothing distraction. Pulling over to take in the panoramic view and breathe the fresh ocean air was tempting, but time was ticking. Soon we turned off the highway and arrived at the beige one-story medical building. Seemingly untouched since the seventies, it needed a makeover, as did the sparse and dated waiting room. Basic metal chairs lined the neutral walls. I'd likely be treated by a no-nonsense doctor with decades of experience practicing in this same spot. That was good, right?

As my name was called to see the doctor, my challenge was getting there on crutches without being stopped for a Breathalyzer. I hadn't gotten the hang of them yet. Sherpa Tom carried my sweater, hat, scarf, oversized handbag, X-rays and my specialist referral. Without the referral, I would have been billed for my visit at a higher rate. Tom bundled everything inside my sweater, knotting the sleeves. If I got tripped up on my crutches, he said he'd toss the bundle on the floor to cushion my fall. *Ha!* Actually Tom was always close enough to catch me, despite his joking around. We followed an aide to an examining room. Where? At the far, far end of the hall—perfect for patients with sore feet! A whiff of germicides, adhesives and bandages let me know that this wasn't a flower shop.

Tom: As Joan carefully eased off her bedroom slipper, Doctor Two Potato, the podiatrist, entered the long, narrow examining room. If he rolled a bowling ball, it could have knocked us both over. He was short and stocky, about sixty, with straight black hair and a stud earring. His open collar revealed curly grey chest hairs peeking out and tangling around a heavy gold chain. Unlike many doctors, he was on time. He greeted us with a somewhat friendly, but authoritative attitude. I sat quietly with Joan's handbag on my lap, a new look for me.

Joan: I briefly explained how I had hurt myself as the doctor examined my sausage-shaped foot. After my loud yelp, Dr. Two Potato recorded my pain level at NINE on a one-to-ten scale, and noted that my foot couldn't support any weight. I handed him my X-rays taken earlier at the Health Center. After a quick glance he tossed them aside. Annoyed, he said they were taken in a reclining position, which is incorrect and worthless. He made clear that he had told them that before. Instead he ordered his own weight-bearing X-rays.

Tom: Joan may have lucked out here, I thought. The guy knew what he wanted, including pitch black hair at sixty.

Joan: Dr. Two Potato explained that weight-bearing X-rays showed the foot in its functional position. Weight bearing caused deformities to become more apparent and easier to diagnose. Misaligned bones became more obvious. That made sense. What didn't was how he expected to get a weight-bearing X-ray when he'd noted that I couldn't put any weight on my foot.

Simple. In Radiology, they're called stress X-rays. I was directed to stand on an X-ray plate, and it HURT—several times for different views. Stepping up to the plate was the painful price I had to pay to get a good picture of what I believed had happened—something tore or snapped.

Tom: It seemed sadistic, but I guess it was pain for gain. More concerning was Joan using her crutches as she was taken to X-ray. Crutches require balance, dexterity, and upper body strength and should come with a video. As I watched from our examining room doorway, a nightmare scenario unfolded. Joan and another patient, both apparently new to crutches, had to pass each other in the narrow hallway. Hard not to laugh as each stopped suddenly urging, "You first!" "No, you first!" Both then went first and yes, collided. No damage, no exchange of identification.

It wasn't long before my wincing and distracted wife hopped back in through the doorway. One of her crutches caught the leg of a flimsy wire display rack sending everything flying. Joan moved as though her crutches were tipped with banana peels! I grabbed her so she wouldn't fall, and marionetted her over the orthotic debris field of insoles, heel cushions and toenail clippers. After helping her onto the examining table, I picked up the stuff and neatly restocked the rack, compulsive that I am. I returned to my chair, wedged between Joan on the table and huge wall cabinets. If the cabinet doors were left open, I'd probably be trapped in a fire.

Joan: My murky looking X-rays were now open on Dr. Two Potato's computer. Were these the *better* images he needed?! Fortunately it wasn't my job to read the blurry marks and black blobs. They looked like a Rorschach Test—anything you wanted them to be. Again a smiling doctor announced there were no fractures. "That's good," he said, "because foot fractures take six weeks to heal." I remember him saying, "Nothing broken, nothing torn." That was good news, but what was causing all the pain and swelling?

Dr. Two Potato examined my foot as he dictated to his assistant. Sprain of left foot...contusion of left ankle, and things like sprain of some unspecified ligament of my left ankle, contusion of my left foot, swelling and bruising across the underside of my midfoot. Strangely, it wasn't like most amoeba-shaped bruises. It was a straight, unswerving burgundy band, about two inches wide, running from one side to the other. It was orderly and tightly controlled—an anal-retentive bruise if Freud were describing it.

Tom: As a nod to Joan's art degree, her burgundy bruise seemed like an unfinished Mark Rothko color field painting. Two or three adjoining bands of color are characteristic of those works. Some say they evoke feelings of awe or transcendence. Though Joan's bruise was a color band short of being artistically complete, what it evoked was clear—something that hurt like hell!!

I had never broken any bones or torn anything, but I did get several sprained ankles playing basketball. The sprains hurt, puffed up some and made me limp for a week or so. They didn't look anything like Joan's foot, though, with its odd pattern of swelling and discoloration. I was glad the doc felt that her injury wasn't serious—surprised too.

14

Joan: Dr. Two Potato wrapped my foot in a semi-rigid cast, told me to ice and elevate it three times a day, and assured me that I'd be fine. "Fine" was exactly what I wanted to hear. His sweet young aide was told to fit me for a walking boot, and I was told to return in two weeks. He said I could walk in my cast and boot, letting pain be my guide.

Tom: Since he didn't write a prescription, I asked what Joan could take for pain. "Tylenol or any acetaminophen," he said. I knew we had a bottle of ibuprofen at home and asked if that would be okay. "No!" he said firmly. "Ibuprofen is an NSAID, and they've been associated with heart attacks and strokes. We've been advised to stop recommending them."

"I've been using them for years," I said in disbelief.

"You're lucky you're still here to talk about it," he said quizzically, as he handed us off to his aide.

Joan: The aide escorted us down another hallway to one of those never defined small spaces that over time become catch-all storerooms. Cans of tuna, boxes of water and dried fruit sat on dusty shelves as earthquake provisions. Lost and found socks were in another box, and oh, many boxes of boots were piled there too. I wasn't familiar with a walking boot or its unique design. I was tired, still aching and not so clear-headed. The lighting was dim and the boot she placed in front of me was solid black, about eight inches high, and reinforced with black strapping. She asked me to slide my foot into it. I tried but pain made it impossible to negotiate the ninety-degree turn to the bottom. "No problem, you need a larger size," she announced.

Tom: Just what a woman loves to hear when shoe shopping. At least she didn't call it the BIGFOOT model.

Joan: Next she handed over a knee-high boot, much higher and much longer. With difficulty I was able to inch down into it and tentatively push my mega-foot flat to the bottom. "That one fits perfectly," she chirped.

My boot was a few inches longer than my foot, so maybe she was allowing for ... growth??? Or could those extra inches protect my set-back toes from bumps and restless legs of table mates? I was sad. No one offered me a lollipop or a cookie. *Meh-schmeh-dontcare.* With the cast, boot, crutches, and Tom there for support—my purse on his arm—we trudged out of the office in my Frankenstein footwear.

Tom: A bolt through Joan's neck would have completed the look. But this was hardly the time to shop for accessories. We headed home so Joan could ice her foot and rest, but not 'til after a surprising discovery.

CHAPTER THREE

Light Bulb Moment

Joan: Once home, inside the boot box I found instructions and diagrams of my black boot. It identified rows of adjustable horizontal black straps spaced from the toes up to the knee. Guided by the illustrations, and after a brain blink moment, it all became clear. I pulled open several rough Velcro straps, and then separated both sides of the boot outward. Yay! That opened a space so wide that I could lift my foot straight up and out from the sole of the boot. Then to put it back on, I could lower my foot straight down onto it without bending my ankle, and fasten the sides back together. So simple and well designed! I also learned that when I pressed a red ball on the side, the liner inside the boot would inflate so my foot wouldn't have too much wiggle room.

If only the aide had a clue! In fairness, she did say it was her first day there. Problem was, it was my first day there too. With most new hires these days, they're expected to figure things out for themselves. Just a few hours would have fully trained this employee. Someone must have decided it wasn't worth those few hours of training because she might up and leave some time before retirement.

Decisions about office management are made from the top down. When I got home and figured out how the boot worked, I was happy and relieved. Looking back, I should have questioned the aide's inexperience, and wondered whether other things at the office were as haphazard.

Velcro is a curious partnership of many tiny interlocking hooks and loops that open and close quickly. The sound of velcro straps being pulled apart was disturbing. I asked Tom if he had an unpleasant emotional reaction to it. Rip, slit, slash, split,—it was almost as though my skin were being ripped apart. Crazy but it felt real!

Tom: I told her to cut back on the slasher films. Joan and I were given windbreakers recently by a tour company as thanks for taking one of their trips. They closed with velcro. You didn't open them during a movie or church service unless you liked getting the stink eye. Velcro ripping as well as accidentally stepping on your cat's tail are among unsettling sounds you don't want to hear. Just behind velcro is hearing your grown child say he wants to move back in with you ... along with his wife, three kids and a Great Dane.

Joan: At home, Tom continually made batches of ice cubes, and every four hours filled ice packs for my foot. Dr. Two Potato had told me to ice my foot for fifteen minutes at a time. Even after thirty or more minutes, I couldn't feel any cold getting through the thick wrapping of his soft cast. Under the doctor's bandages, my foot and ankle were not only swollen, but now also hot.

Tom: My job got more challenging. Each ice treatment required lots of cubes. Seemed that Dr. Two Potato turned a blind eye to his soft cast cold barrier. A dozen ice cube-laying penguins couldn't keep up with the demand. A phone call to our healer brought reassurance that the cold was indeed penetrating and doing its job, regardless of how it felt. Just proves you can learn something every day. Joan's *hot* foot was actually cold. I felt lukewarm about that.

Joan: Even with crutches and the boot, my foot hurt if I put any weight on it. I wanted to resume normal activities like cooking, the glitch being that I needed one hand for each crutch. Not only was preparing meals on crutches a minefield, but in a few days my arms and shoulders ached from lifting my own weight with each step.

Tom: I tried to persuade Joan to give her sore body a break. I told her I could make breakfast. I'd just google how to open cereal boxes and slice a banana. And for lunch, I was sure YouTube had videos on making a sandwich. She laughed and relented.

Joan: Tom even offered to bring in dinners. Actually he insisted. He didn't have to do that, I told him. The clincher was when he added coffee ice cream for dessert.

It was nice to be waited on, but I started feeling like a wimp. I had been told there was no fracture and I'd get better soon, so I felt like I was taking advantage of Tom. After a few days I tried to fix meals again, sometimes on an office chair that rolled, sometimes asking for Tom's help with the legwork from refrigerator to prep area, from prep area to stovetop or oven, and from pantry to microwave to table. I felt I had to toughen up, and in my ginormous boot and crutches, try not to trip on the road to recovery.

TIP #3: Put your medical paperwork in a large folder, ideally with pockets or dividers which can also hold a pen and notepad. Referrals, test results, care instructions, co-pays, receipts, appointment dates, and insurance phone numbers go in the folder. Keep your own notes about what took place at each appointment. Tape the doctor's business card on the front, as well as the cards for any associates. This folder will expand like yeast dough on a warm day.

Notes about doctor visit dates, tests and whatever was done at each office visit will help later when you pair up visits, bills and payments. Buy about 10,000 staples to start.

TIP #4: As your care continues, request copies of any X-rays, MRIs and CT scans for your folder. Usually just the report is sufficient. Only one radiology department collected $10 for a disc with copies of X-rays. Having them will help if you go to another doctor for a second opinion.

CHAPTER FOUR

Nursed Through a Straw

Joan: We were back for my follow-up visit. It was good that Dr. Two Potato's office door didn't close with velcro, or else his boot fitter wouldn't know how to get in or out. Things changed on this second visit. After a long wait, we heard a patient complaining loudly about how long he had been sitting there. He shouted he would leave if he wasn't seen immediately. I was also bugged, but with my bad foot, I was hardly able to stomp out too.

Vulnerability and fear immediately after an accident may cause people to doctor shop for the one who can see them soonest. Unfortunately some doctors may make a grab for new patients, squeezing them in no matter what. A newly injured patient could generate six, eight, or ten future visits—a nice cash flow. Existing patients were unlikely to leave and start over with someone new.

Tom: Our Health Center doesn't double-book patients, but unfortunately it has become standard practice in many medical offices. If someone didn't show up, there was always another insurance payment waiting. Some doctors, though, don't stop there. When referred to a specialist a few years ago, I waited well over an hour with a bunch of restless patients. We took a poll and found that four of us had the same appointment time. Now back to our story, "Waiting for Two Potato."

An hour and twenty minutes passed before he appeared. He entered in a rush with no explanation. It's curious how people who show up late are always in a hurry. My Grandma would have twisted his ear 'til he remembered his manners.

Joan: An apology would have been nice, but my referral said he was a Podiatrist. Nice wasn't listed. Still feeling grateful for how he squeezed me in the day after my accident, I ignored his boorishness because I needed him to focus on my foot. I told him it still hurt and I couldn't put weight on it. He nodded as he cut through the layers of my soft cast. He noted there was less swelling … more flexibility … and said the pain would gradually diminish. Yes, the swelling had decreased some since I last saw him. That made it more obvious that the inner side of my midfoot was bulging outward (like the curved bracket at the end of these parentheses) instead of the normal curve inward. Alarmed, I said, "It looks worse now than before!" With a confident bearing, he encouraged me not to worry. He calmly explained that besides badly spraining my ankle, I had injured other parts of my foot, and the bulging area was still swollen.

He unwrapped an elastic ankle brace for me to wear for support. The smell of this stretchy, rubbery sleeve bounced off the vinegary smell of different adhesives—clean but not a fragrance I wanted to smell like. He instructed me to keep icing and elevating to reduce the puffiness and bruising. I wasn't aware that icing could be effective so long after an injury, but was eager to do whatever might help. Overall my foot was improving, he said, with eyes that were disengaged. "Good to know," I replied, grabbing hold of any encouragement. Who doesn't want to believe the best of a painful situation? Looking back, it was like being offered a small sample of chocolate at Costco, making it likely I'd return for more.

Tom: There was an odd mix of attention and detachment in Dr. Two Potato. Despite some snarly moments, he was optimistic, reassuring and downplayed Joan's fears. Those positive words were clearly delivered but with emotional distance. The smile arrived on schedule, but the feeling behind it missed the train. It seemed that as a baby, he had been nursed through a straw.

Joan: Over the next several weeks, my ballooned foot resembled those live Doppler weather maps on TV. Colors appeared, migrated, then faded as other colors bloomed. At my next visit, even though the overall swelling had decreased slightly, my foot still hurt as much. Also, that bulge on the side of my foot hadn't changed. Dr. Two Potato remained positive and again shrugged off my concerns.

Tom: Because of a doctor's aura of knowledge and authority, he can get away with stuff a husband never could. If I casually blew off Joan's questions and concerns, I'd be sleeping in the den, and not getting paid for my opinion.

Joan: It had been Dr. Two Potato's experience, he confided, that recovery time from bad sprains was hard to predict, but eventually things normalized. Keep icing and elevating, he advised while strapping my foot with athletic tape for support. I got the feeling my mouth might get strapped too if I asked why the pain hadn't gradually diminished like he said it would.

Tom: Neither Joan nor I remembered when plantar fasciitis was added to the diagnosis. Dr. Two Potato, the Podiatrist, henceforth referred to as Dr. Two Pot-Pod, mentioned it offhandedly while taping her foot differently. Joan kept saying that she felt pain from the bottom of her foot, curving around the inner side and onto the top. She thought the plantar fascia ran along the bottom of the foot in a heel to toe direction. Seemed that the Doc's GPS was off. But Joan said she landed hard after her leap from the boulder, so it was possible the plantar fascia was injured too.

23

Joan's diagnoses seemed to be evolving, but how many original diagnoses on TV medical shows turn out to be what a patient was finally treated for? Maybe the Doc wasn't the best communicator, but he had treated foot and ankle problems for years. He was a foot specialist and I wasn't.

Joan: Over the years, medical care has become extremely specialized with each doctor performing a narrowly focused set of skills. I had worked for a group of medical specialists, but there had never been a podiatrist in my department. I had no background in this specialty, neither in college nor in nursing practice. When I got injured, I had the same worries and concerns as other patients.

At a follow-up exam, Dr. Two Pot Pod pressed different points on my foot asking for my reaction. I told him the weird lump on the inner side of my midfoot still hurt. Continuing his exam, he said my foot was swollen but definitely improving ... my pain level was lower, and after bending my foot and toes in various ways, said I had more mobility. I agreed that it was less swollen and it did hurt a bit less, but—interrupting, he reminded me that no two patients recover at the same rate.

His partial reinforcement kept me coming back, but a long time had passed without appreciable improvement. It was getting harder to feel encouraged when he kept stressing that I was getting better. "Ice and elevate" he kept saying, while even the glaciers were running low on ice. As we left, mixed messages popped in and out of our heads. Tom and I struggled with reassurance/uncertainty, optimism/angst and confidence/confusion. The eight of us piled into the car and tried to make sense of it.

Weeks passed with little improvement. My foot was still puffy, still hurt, and was still bruised on the top and bottom. Watching me limp, our daughter suggested getting a second opinion to put all of our minds at rest. That would have made sense, except that over the years, our Health Center had always referred us to competent specialists. Some we liked more than others, but they were all well-qualified, so why wouldn't Dr. Two Pot-Pod also be, despite his quirks?

Tom: Using baseball as an example, we didn't want to believe that our hitting streak of good referrals would end. Our daughter, however, felt it had ended and suggested a pinch hitter. Being hung up on our winning streak, we kept the same batter in the game. Looking back, it seemed like a decision made after getting hit on the head by a foul ball.

Joan: So much time had gone by since my accident that by my next visit, I was worn and weary. Maybe he was too, so he dropped the reassurances and ordered more X-rays—additional views this time. The new smudgy images showed something different—a small Lisfranc ligament tear. I was surprised, but strangely relieved! X-rays finally showed an injury where my foot had been hurting! Great news!

Tom: Joan was relieved that the source of her pain was finally identified. Suddenly there was hope, but also a big question: why hadn't he found this earlier? He pointed out that a Lisfranc injury is uncommon, far from the first thing you look for. He was not at all defensive, just pleased with his discovery after months of looking for pain in all the wrong places.

Joan: This tear was minor, he assured us, and would repair itself. I definitely didn't need surgery, he said. I was told to continue icing and elevating, and I'd be fine. When Dr. Two Pot-Pod dictated his notes and said the word Lisfranc, I heard *Liz Frank*, a woman's name. She sounded less clinical, more personal. I could relate to her. We were partners. My pain was her pain, and she more than anyone understood what was going on—it really hurt.

Dr. Two Pot-Pod said he was going away on vacation. I imagined he was going to climb Mt. Everest where there's nothing but *ice and elevation*. An MRI was ordered, authorized, and I had it done. After he returned from Mt. Everest, or wherever, he said the MRI report showed no additional abnormality, not even the Lisfranc injury was mentioned. What was going on? It was hurting more and there was no reason! Did my original pain imprint a memory trail that I was registering as real when it wasn't? I was still in pain—or crazy—tough call. Dr. Two Pot-Pod reminded me that my recent X-rays showed a small ligament tear and that they are very slow to heal, so I needed to be patient. I told him my intuition led me to believe I needed something other than patience.

Since I was still hurting, out came Dr. Two Pot-Pod's Rx pad. He wrote a scrip for a prescription strength NSAID, an anti-inflammatory medicine. On Day One, he had told us there was a risk in using NSAIDs, but after many months together, it seemed he was willing to take that risk! To be kind, we both needed back-up.

Tom: Mixed message time! The doc didn't recommend NSAIDs before, then he did. Even if he was bugged that his treatments weren't working, I didn't think he'd want to lose a patient to a heart attack or stroke. With retirement approaching, each additional co-pay could mean a pair of senior dinners at Applebee's without tapping the pension. I'm sure he felt the reward for Joan was greater than the risk.

Joan: Dr. Two Pot-Pod taped my foot again, and for additional support, said to wear orthotics which he sold. He also wrote an order to start Physical Therapy, and our visit was over.

When I was introduced to Kirstie, my physical therapist, I welcomed the opportunity for improvement. Her manner was warm and caring while her voice delivered plainly spoken, clear instructions. For a few weeks, she patiently guided me through exercises, and therapeutically massaged what hurt. PT exercises involved a limited degree of pain, but my foot got somewhat stronger, and my balance improved. Working with Kirstie was helping.

I did my homework exercises diligently, but I still wasn't able to walk longer distances. I wasn't hoping to be a ballerina, but fretted about not being able to lift up on my toes to reach higher shelves. Neither could I do other exercises that would have been easy before my injury. I pressed Kirstie for a recovery time. She acknowledged my concern but said that ligaments took a long time to heal. "How long, Kirstie?" Reluctantly she said maybe as long as six months to a year. "You're kidding?! NO!" I cried out, causing a patient to slide off her balance ball.

During the next few weeks of Physical Therapy, my tootsie became happier. My concern and pain level dropped significantly, and I was happy to be getting better. But was I?

It had seemed that over the past dozen PT visits, Kirstie's work and my best efforts brought improvement. What a shocking awareness when the stabbing pain returned after the pain meds ran out. I hadn't been healing after all. It just seemed that way. The NSAID had masked the pain.

Sad and disheartened, I stopped going to physical therapy.

CHAPTER FIVE

My Third Ankle

Joan: At my next visit, I updated Dr. Two Pot-Pod on the NSAID fiasco. I told him I had worked hard at Physical Therapy. I tried to convince him that something was being missed. That wasn't what he wanted to hear. He became more dismissive of me. Was I a frustrating reminder of his ineffective treatments, or did he think I was a malingering cry baby?

I sensed that my concerns, as well as my presence, were irritating the doctor. But my foot wasn't *fine* as I had been told it would be. My treatment was a fine failure. Up until then, I believed my responsibility was not to assess my care, but to comply with my doctor's advice as best I could. So now he was annoyed with me?! Well, I was annoyed with him too! I asked him again, this time bluntly, "Why does the inner side of my midfoot feel hard and why is it still protruding?" He wagged his head back and forth and said he had already told me it was swollen. Continue the icing and elevating, he suggested with a pooh-poohing shrug.

Enough, no more of his coddiwompling! After five months of treatment, what was sticking out sideways didn't feel soft and swollen, rather it felt quite hard. I pointed and asked, "Why is this bone sticking out?" Like a self-assured instructor talking to a slow learner, he said, "That's your ankle, Joan."

Huh? Did he miss nursery school the day everyone learned "Dem Bones, Dem Bones, Dem Dry Bones"? Thinking maybe he misunderstood, I said, "I mean this one," as I pointed to the bulge again. I then tapped on my actual ankle which was three inches away and said, "Not that one." Another shrug along with "I don't know why." No kidding, that's what he said! I was shell-shocked and numb, confronted with the reality that I was on my own.

Tom: Even if he believed all along what he had just said, shouldn't a podiatrist be curious about a patient's extra ankle?

Joan: Tchyeah! Dazed and disillusioned, Tom and I walked out trying to come to terms with what we had just heard. In the car it fully hit us that we, *Mister and Miss-Diagnosed,* had been taken for a ride that went nowhere. Incredible! *Aarrgh!*

TIP #5: Persistent doubts along with unanswered questions may be a signal to see another doctor. A second opinion could catch an overlooked injury. At the very least, hearing the same diagnosis and treatment plan from someone else would put your mind at ease. A human foot has more than 100 muscles, tendons, and ligaments, 33 joints, and 26 bones. An injury to a tiny part of the foot can be significant since all 159 parts have to work together. Maybe your doctor mastered 158 of them, but if your problem was 159 like mine was, you'll need someone else to diagnose that.

CHAPTER SIX

My Friend Liz Vents

Liz: The name's actually Lisfranc. No, I didn't change my name after moving to L.A. I'm a ligament and I connect a midfoot bone to the second toe.

I've been silent 'til now. But months have been wasted with grab bag therapies for everything, except for what was wrong! My so-called treatment was based on inky X-rays that looked like something an octopus had used for target practice. Dr. Two Pot-Pod should have known his X-rays couldn't tell the whole story about me. Often people think their photo doesn't look like them. On his murky images, I could barely find myself or the fractured bone I had been attached to. That's right, I said "fractured" bone —the fracture he said Joan didn't have! Right, I'm hopping mad-- at least on the good foot!

Ligaments aren't known to have feelings, but I'm torn. I mean really torn—away from Joan's midfoot bone! For God's sake, a piece of bone's still dangling right under the skin! A doctor's dog wouldn't miss that. And I didn't just have a "small tear that would heal itself." It's much worse! How can this doctor act so cocksure while completely missing signals? Am I the only one recognizing his flummadiddle?

A serious Lisfranc injury has classic symptoms: intense pain with midfoot swelling, a purple band under the arch, a distorted foot, bruised instep, inability to stand on toes, and difficulty walking. The symptoms were distinct and lined up as neatly as points on a roadmap. But many men won't look at maps. They claim they know where they're going, until they're lost. Then they still won't ask. What other clues did he need to diagnose this? Runway lights blinking all the way down Joan's leg to the injury?

Why has he diminished and disregarded me? I've been put at risk here. Joan was told it's safe to keep walking on her foot. It wasn't, but she's not yet aware of all that's really wrong. I don't know how much more damage I can take. If his patient isn't showing much improvement after months, why doesn't he refer her to another doctor for a second opinion? Who am I kidding? Then his fragile ego might take a hit. I hope there's someone else who can help!

CHAPTER SEVEN

Tom Mansplaining

Tom: Joan's ligament was very upset. She had a right to be! Is it really hard to imagine a body part with feelings and language? The actual language may not be like ours, but it can deliver a clear message. You fall off a bike onto your arm, and your arm tells you it hurts. A crooked arm tells you to see a doctor. The knot in your stomach tells you it's expensive. Lots of messages.

Frat boys order a pledge to touch a hot stove for as long as he's told. He obeys as sensory receptors shoot signals to his brain, which interprets them as pain. His brain signals back to move his schmuck-knuckled hand away. The pledge chooses whether to listen to his brain or his brainless mentors.

A kid walks past candy bars in a market. No one's looking, so he slips one in his pocket. As he starts to leave, he feels anxious. His stomach starts churning. Something inside is telling him it's wrong. Our body's like a broadcasting station speaking mainly to us. We just have to tune in. While we might be crazy if we talk to ourselves, we're always wise if we listen.

If your heartbeat stutters, is it sa-saying something? You bet, and an EKG machine can translate the message. For a long time we humans needed a keyboard to *speak* to our computer. Now we can use voice recognition. We're getting closer to when all the parts of our bodies will be speaking to us via devices, or with other energies we don't yet know we have.

Our body is amazing. It can receive scary messages through its fears, happy messages through its ears, send sad messages with its tears, and in moments of passion, relay a message that's quite uplifting.

The feelings of the ligament that Joan calls *Liz are* important to this story. As Joan's kindred spirit in a sisterhood of pain, Liz has an interesting history. "Lisfranc" was actually the name of a surgeon in Napoleon's army. He was first to perform a very risky operation around a then-unnamed ligament. The surgery was successful, so in tribute, the ligament was given his name. Two hundred years later *Liz* was in another battle, and her life was at stake once again.

CHAPTER EIGHT

Relationship on Ice

Joan: A clear strategy for what to do next was elusive. A yogi might encourage students to focus on their third eye. Instead I found myself staring meditatively at my *third* ankle for long periods. It was as though doing that would make it fix itself or reveal the cure. It didn't, but what staring did was clear my mind and help me focus on what to do next.

I gathered up my pain and disillusionment for a visit back to my internist, only to learn he wasn't available. He recommended another doctor with whom I shared my recent history. Tom and I liked Doctor Three Potato's manner, and were grateful for Dr. One Potato's endorsement. Alert and intellectually curious, he had a laser focus on what I was saying. He was puzzled why the podiatrist still had me icing and elevating five months after my injury. He said it's only effective the first few days. Tom and I sighed in unison.

Dr. Three Potato shook his head in dismay, and submitted a referral for me to see an orthopedic foot and ankle specialist. Orthopedic doctors require specialized imaging, a cast room and supplies specific to their needs. Foot and ankle doctors are a relatively new subspecialty in orthopedics. A sub-specialist is a specialist of a subspecialty. Well, that clears that up! Foot and ankle surgeons now treat many of the same conditions as podiatrists, but referring physicians often don't associate orthopedic surgeons with treatment of foot/ankle problems. Luckily my new internist did.

Tom: I did a quick icing calculation. Figuring a minimum of fifteen minutes, three times a day for five months, Joan had frittered away more than 6,750 minutes under ice. Only dead mastodons have been under ice longer. Joan's 6,750 minutes on ice computed to 112.5 hours. A non-stop flight from Los Angeles to Antarctica takes eighteen and a quarter hours. Joan could have taken three round-trip flights to Antarctica and still have had three hours to plunk her foot on an iceberg. It would have been cold enough to penetrate Two Pot-Pod's cast, while Joan could joyfully take pictures of penguins!

Joan: Starting over was my only choice, but I became concerned about the impact this was having on Tom. Because of my mistake, his life had taken an abrupt turn. He showed no dissatisfaction or resentment, only support. Still, he became heir to unfamiliar and worrisome tasks without the gratification of seeing improvement on my part. Would he reach the logical point of "Why bother?" I'd seen some marriages fail under the stress of long-term illness. The thought didn't escape me. I wanted my marriage to survive.

TIP #6: In my medical training, knowledge took priority over feelings. I had been trained to listen to my brain. Nevertheless, there was a guiding force beyond my rational mind. It was like a second brain. In my *gut*, I thought something was wrong when Dr. Two Pot-Pod didn't. My *gut* had been calling out to me while I tried not to pay attention. Trust yourself. If needed, talk to your primary care doctor about redirecting your care.

CHAPTER NINE

Pinpoint Accuracy

Tom: Dr. Four Potato, Joan's new orthopedic sub-specialist, was tall, mid-50's and fit. He had a military bearing, but a peacekeeper's warmth. Direct and straightforward, he made us feel like Joan's interminable problem would soon have a solution. We liked him right off.

Joan: It took a while to get an appointment, but Doctor Four Potato was worth the wait. He reviewed copies I brought of my MRI report and my X-rays on disc. I summarized my care, and asked whether he could tell me what was wrong. He politely asked permission to do one new X-ray before discussing that.

Afterward he gathered Tom and me 'round the digital image on his computer. He described my injury and showed us where a ligament tore and yanked off a piece of bone. Hearing that, Tom cringed and sucked air through his clenched teeth as he pulled his shoulders tight. Just as sounds can awaken images and emotions, witnessing and talking about another's injuries can create physical pain in the observer/listener. Tom's wincing while experiencing my pain happened because of a remarkable thing called *neural resonance*. The mirror neurons, cells in our brains, handle that. They help people feel empathy for others. Tom was feeling empathy as well as some temporary deafness as his hands covered his ears.

Tom: I remembered gasping when the doctor described Joan's injury, but not pulling my shoulders tight or covering my ears. Maybe it was a defense mechanism to keep from hearing more. Yet I did remember how what he said made me feel. I shuddered with a nauseating chill in my stomach. Emotionally distracted, I think I missed most of the following explanation.

Joan: Finally everything started making sense. I did not have just a small tear that Dr. Two Pot-Pod said would heal on its own. Unlike his X-rays that appeared to be shot through Beijing's pollution, Dr. Four Potato's X-ray machine produced such a sharp bright image that I clearly saw and understood the problem. After my ligament tore, Dr. Four Potato explained, there was nothing to hold my midfoot bones in place. They slid sideways, explaining the bulge I had repeatedly asked Dr. Two Pot-Pod about—a.k.a. my third ankle. Dr. Four Potato diagnosed a *Distinct Lisfranc Fracture Displacement.* Again I heard *Liz Frank.* She was becoming more personal. Liz was a part of me and had been hurting. Dr. Four Potato said to think of the past five months as water under the bridge. That bridge took a big toll that I wouldn't get back. Yet with Dr. Four Potato's guidance, I started feeling hopeful about getting better.

Tom: Joan had been a registered nurse and understood the doctor's lingo. I however had gone to a Jesuit high school. I was required to take four years of Latin and three years of ancient Greek. I remember being told that this Classical Education would prepare me for life. True—life 2,000 years ago. Then in college it was TV and Journalism. Having learned about nothing that remotely required a band-aid, I asked Dr. Four Potato for a translation.

Simply put, he said that a *Lisfranc Fracture Displacement* meant that a particular ligament in Joan's foot was torn, and a bone was broken. Displacement meant that bones in her foot shifted and could only be repositioned by surgery. That simplified explanation helped.

It goes to show that even the most complicated concepts or stories can be understood when they're reduced to simple terms. Another that comes to mind is the classic Greek story of Oedipus, who killed his father so he could marry his mother ... but not until he did his chores. There was more to it, but that was the essence.

Joan: Dr. Four Potato pointed to a chart showing how the Lisfranc ligament runs between the midfoot (medial cuneiform bone in medical language) toward the base of the second toe (second metatarsal bone). He added with a twinkle of amusement that if you drew a line across the ligaments where the other toes join the midfoot, the Lisfranc ligament would *not* be in line with them because "the big toe wants to be a thumb!"

For hitch-hiking? Nah, it's probably a vestige of our tree-swinging days when an opposable thumb could separate from the other toes to grasp things. I was amused with this tale. My monkey tail had long disappeared so I was okay with the rest of the evolutionary reference. It's relaxing when a doctor is not so serious that—"*Owwwwwww!* What happened?"

One outstretched finger moved away from my foot. Dr. Four Potato had pressed one specific spot on my foot that sent spasms of intense pain through my body and back out, like a momentary seizure. I quivered briefly from the sudden jolt I hadn't seen coming. Just as well, because anticipating it would have been unnerving too. From his X-ray, he knew the exact location of my trouble spot, and confirmed it with a single finger poke. It was a low-tech but effective diagnostic tool. His pinpoint accuracy was agonizing but unmistakably reassuring.

Tom: I was reluctant to shake hands with him at the end of our visit, for fear he'd find a sore spot.

Joan: For a CT scan, the patient would be lying down. Because bone and foot alignment change with weight-bearing, Dr. Four Potato wanted a standing PedCAT scan to further confirm his diagnosis. This scan provided a three-dimensional view of Dr. Four Potato's diagnosis, and also the image needed to plan the surgical repair. I liked and respected Dr. Four Potato and his staff, and Tom and I felt comfortable with him as my surgeon.

Surprise! He recommended another surgeon, a female colleague, to perform the operation. He said she would do a better job for this particular surgery because her hands were smaller than his, but strong and dexterous. As a musician, he said, she had highly developed muscles and coordination in her hands. He said they were well-suited for the tight spaces where my injuries were located. I felt like that last unclaimed bag on a luggage carousel, circling endlessly without a resolution. My file was expanding as a referral to yet another doctor was generated and approved.

Tom: We've all heard at least once that such and such doctor acts like he's God. I've never heard a doctor admit that someone else might be better at doing the same thing he does. It took a very secure, competent person to say that, rather than acting like God and having no one to look up to. Still, his recommendation was disorienting, as we were asked to transfer our confidence in him to a fifth doctor. Yes, it was great that she had nimble and muscular hands. I pictured her at the gym chinning herself with her pinkies. So much for fantasy. She did sound capable, and Dr. Four Potato certainly had earned Joan's trust.

Joan: It's true. My alleged plantar fasciitis had evaporated. Poof! My purported third ankle was clearly bogus! I needed to decide whether I should take another halting step, this time to a physician/musician, whose office was thirty miles away.

CHAPTER TEN

Doctor Five Potato to the Rescue

Joan: Because I trusted Dr. Four Potato, and he trusted her, I made an appointment to see Dr. Five Potato. Another week, another doctor! Confidence ruled the day when we met Dr. Five Potato. I gave her my history, but *didn't* mention my imaginary friend, *Liz Frank*, because she might have referred *Liz* and me to yet another kind of doctor.

Tom: As long as Joan didn't chat with her ligament when we were with friends, no problem. I went to meet Dr. Five Potato too. The eyes on this Potato were alert and focused. She radiated competence and professionalism. Maybe she'd laugh if someone tickled her long enough, but that didn't matter. What did was that she maintained eye contact, listened intently, reviewed Dr. Four Potato's diagnosis and Joan's scan, then said exactly what she would do and why.

Joan: No wasted words in Dr. Five Potato's office—only clear, concise information about the required fusion procedure and recovery. When the injury happened, it could have been repaired with what's called a fixation procedure, she said. Bones would have been repositioned, the tough fibrous bands of ligament could have healed and held these bones together. However, in my case additional damage had been done as arthritis had developed over the six months of irritation from walking on displaced bones—the ones Dr. Two Pot-Pod had called *swelling*. Now Dr. Five Potato needed to do a fusion surgery instead. Whatever remained of the ligament, as well as any arthritis, would be totally scraped away. Then adjoining bones would be repositioned and held in place by hardware instead of the ligament. Over time the bones would fuse together into one.

From my surgeon's point of view, as I understood it, additional delay would give rise to more work chiseling and scooping arthritic debris. For me, that would involve more time under anesthesia. Tom and I quickly agreed to the surgery. A referral was submitted to insurance and approved.

My fusion surgery would involve an eight-week, no weight-bearing recovery. *Oh Funkel! Ugh!* There would be no steel bars, no locked cell door, but the sentence for my reckless behavior, jumping off a boulder, was two months of doctor-ordered house arrest!

Tom: Actually Doctor Two Pot-Pod was the one who should have been confined and forced to re-read his podiatry books. But for us it was more energizing to move forward with optimism than dwell on the past. Besides if we kept looking back, we'd bump into things and not notice the good stuff up ahead.

Joan: Since I was having left foot surgery, I asked Dr. Five Potato if she could fix a failed bunion operation done in 2001. It still ached. It was on the little toe of the same foot. She said the surgery previously performed on my bunion was outdated, and it's done differently now. Wouldn't it be great, I thought purposefully out loud, to have both repairs done at he same time? "Not really," Dr. Five Potato responded firmly, "given the amount of trauma you'll have from the Lisfranc fusion surgery."

On the flip side, if I wanted to have the bunion surgery sometime after the fusion surgery, I'd become a serial shut-in, leaving home only for medical appointments. I'd have to stay off the same foot again for who knew how long. Dr. Five Potato warned me that I'd hate her if she did both surgeries together because of the pain afterwards.

Tom: Sometimes you can accomplish with humor what you can't with reason. So I took a shot at it. I turned and said pointedly, "Joan, maybe you shouldn't rush things. Why don't you wait 'til you're 80? You could skip your dental appointments 'cause you might not have any teeth by then. And you'll probably forget your other appointments." A moment later, Joan and our take-charge Doc burst out laughing! "Okay, I'll do both," she agreed, regaining control of the room.

Joan: Tom came through for me. The doctor's assistant submitted the referral for surgery and gave me a "to do" folder containing three prescriptions. One was for pain, of which I'd have plenty, I was again reminded. A second was for constipation from the pain meds—so the side effects were backside effects. The third was for itching, from I'm not sure what. My surgery was a week off, but getting the prescriptions filled right away gave me time to crack the code on opening child-proof containers.

Kid-lets figured out how to get at candy-colored pills by pushing down on the lid while turning it, so that's old school now. Instead it's a two-factor, two-handed operation. Hold the container in the left hand, and push down on the tab with the left thumb while turning the lid with the right. Got it? Once the childproof container was open, with no children having access to the meds, I turned the lid upside down before closing. Next time I was able to get to the pills the old fashioned way. Opening my prescription bottles before I was groggy, disoriented or in pain after surgery was a good call.

Tom: At times I couldn't help wondering how many children got exposed to pills by having to open prescription bottles for their parents. Kids are glad to teach their parents new things, like how to use all the features on their smart phones and TV's, except Parental Controls. As for opening pill bottles, it's better to ask your pharmacist.

Joan: In the folder there was also a doctor's order for rental of a two-part medical device: one part for Cold Therapy, the other a DVT (Deep Vein Thrombosis) compression unit to use after surgery. Cold therapy would pump ice water down to a pouch placed inside my cast to relieve pain and prevent swelling, while the DVT unit prevented blood clots from forming.

When your doctor orders a medical device, check with your insurance company for the names of medical supply companies that are covered by your insurance. Add the date and names of people you spoke with to your folder.

I was also given a doctor's order for a steerable knee scooter. Streamers flowing from the handlebars were optional. We gave these devices immediate attention so they could be delivered before my surgery. Hallelujah! No referrals necessary!

I never had a scooter when I was a kid, so here was my chance, even with Toys R Us going belly up! I was told that after surgery, I should plant my good foot on the ground and lift my casted leg to kneel on the sheepskin-covered knee platform. My good foot would propel me forward. At twenty-six pounds, the scooter was described as lightweight and easily transported. Funny images raced through my mind. First image—there I was riding my scooter to my car. Second blurry image—there I was balancing on one foot trying to lift the scooter into the trunk. Third—there I was on the ground with the scooter on top of me. No, my scooter would not be "easily transported."

Tom: Joan's Scooter wrangler to the rescue! For doctor visits, I secured Joan's wheels in the back of my SUV, cushioning it from scratches! No tipping please! I love my work.

Joan: A nice bonus was receiving a signed form authorizing a three-month Disabled Person Parking Placard in case I halfwittedly decided to go clubbing with my broken foot. AAA handed me my placard in minutes versus hours at the Department of Motor Vehicles. Except for two doctor visits, the placard stayed in my purse. It had expired by the time I was ready to drive anywhere by myself.

TIP #7: If your insurance doesn't cover the rental of your medical devices, you can pick up donated devices at hospital gift shops, Salvation Army or Saint Vincent de Paul. Shopping at these or other organizations would be cost saving to you while the charity also would benefit from the sale. Look around while you're there. You may find some Corning Ware pieces to replace the ones that splintered on your tile floor. I'm not pointing fingers, it happens.

CHAPTER ELEVEN

Job Retraining for Tom

Joan: I was advised to eat more protein and iron-rich foods after surgery, and get extra calcium to aid in healing. I understood the concept but would be dependent on Tom for meals. He would be waiting on me hand and foot, mostly foot, not an easy task for a novice in the kitchen.

Tom: "Novice" was a polite description. I had visited our kitchen on many occasions—nice room—and usually left with a drink or snack. Now a near-alien world of modern appliances with thick manuals awaited—manuals I had placed neatly in labeled file pockets of different colors, along with research from the internet about key features that each appliance should have. After delivery, my job was done. I proudly presented this package to Joan without reading a word. *Whataguy!*

Joan: Meal prep after surgery would be problematic, so I began doubling dinner recipes. The uneaten halves were frozen in pyrex containers to be reheated as I recovered. I quickly ran out of containers. Then I realized that once solidly frozen, the meals could be transferred to freezer bags, making the containers available for a fill-up. The container to plastic bag system was repeated, providing convenient meals for the newbie to serve during my immediate post-op period.

Tom: I asked Joan to shove a stick in each frozen meal, so on hot days we could just lick 'em. She took aim and squirted me with Reddi-wip. Right, my just desserts. I really appreciated her thinking ahead and providing ready-made dinners. They eased my transition into preparing dinners myself. Lunches I felt I could handle. You can't burn a salad. Cereal and cut-up fruits were easy, and I already knew how to make Joan's favorite breakfast—oatmeal with blueberries. I watched her make it a few times and wrote down all the measurements and steps. Only a million more light years to my Michelin Star!

Actually I had a tad of cooking experience when the kids were little. On Sunday mornings, I'd fry bacon or an eastern breakfast meat called scrapple. We all loved it! Joan's cousin, who was a butcher, described scrapple as all the parts of a pig that went over a fence last. Don't sneer. Hot dogs and sausages have jumped that fence too. But seasoned with spices and fried 'til the outsides were crisp, scrapple was a taste treat for former Philadelphians. Pass the ketchup please!

For many, making dinner is right out of "Cooking 101." For me it was 911. What did I need to do, in what order and for how long?! Joan's lessons started calmly with the basics of how to operate our new appliances and deal with their vagaries. I jotted it all in my caregiver notebook—no, not on a smartphone. I didn't want Siri talking smack about me behind my back.

The dishwasher and I already had a relationship since I had made meal clean-up one of my household jobs. The microwave was friendly if I stuck to reheating—a limited but cordial connection. Our toaster oven, however, had ambitions to do far more than toast—like bake, broil and roast. People like that used to annoy me, pretending to be something they're not. But in today's world, people and toasters have had to re-invent themselves, develop new skills. That included me in the kitchen.

Joan: I explained to Chef Tom why one piece of toast required four selections to get started. First, from the eight cooking options, select TOAST. Second, choose from the numerical sequence how light or dark you want it. Third, decide how many slices to toast. Fourth, push the ON switch.

Tom: As I listened to Joan's helpful, encouraging, yes loving how-tos, my *on* switch was pushed too.

Joan: Those extra toaster settings not only provided more options, but were important safety features imposed after the last major earthquake here. During that 6.6 temblor, falling toaster ovens started many fires in Los Angeles. As they slid off countertops, their single ON switch bumped other objects in their path. The toaster ovens switched on, heated up, and burned down houses.

Tom: ... some lighter, some darker. They were toast! (I'm not exactly proud of that thought, but sometimes they just come.)

Joan: I told Tom to forget about broiling, but baking was useful for fish, chicken breasts, even burgers if he didn't barbecue them. The magic number was 350 degrees except for potatoes and salmon at 400.

Tom: I struggled with this. Potatoes were all different sizes. How long was I supposed to bake them? It would help if a potato's eyes closed when it was done. Joan said to squeeze them with a potholder to see whether they were soft. She then gave me a list of foods we usually ate along with approximate cooking times. Approximate—that left things somewhere between undercooked and burnt—still it was better than not eating at all. How could Joan handle living on the edge like that?! My sweet daredevil suggested I buy some packaged foods that had cooking instructions on the label. Great idea! As for beans and asparagus that grow without directions printed on them, I tasted them to see when they were done. For spaghetti and frozen foods, sure enough, the label said it all. I stopped looking for that magic powder that I could mix with water to make Gordon Ramsay materialize and answer questions.

I thought it would be a good idea to watch Joan prepare every meal during the week before her surgery. She said a better idea would be for ME to cook and SHE'D watch. So pushy! She continued with her overview of our kitchen appliances—things to be aware of.

Joan: The *Built-in Electric Convection Double Ovens* turned out large pots of stew in slightly more time than it took to read that mouthful of a name. *The Easy Set Guide* and the *Food Poisoning Hazard Warning* were all I needed to show Tom in the manual he never read.

Tom: Update! I read one page where I learned the nuance between salmon and salmonella. Despite how it sounded, it was not Italian seafood.

Joan: Moving along, bread proofing had to wait 'til my next fracture. As for using the pressure cooker, that lesson could wait too. I didn't want Tom's pressure rising higher than the appliance's.

Tom: A friend of mine who loves to cook told me about the first meal he prepared in a pressure cooker long ago. It was chicken with vegetables in an Italian sauce. Assuming the meal was done, he opened the lid of the pressure cooker before all the pressure had released. His chicken and veggies rocketed up and stuck to the ceiling! Shooting from the rear of the chicken was a contrail of steaming tomato sauce. That was also my friend Phil's last pressure cooker meal.

Joan: Just to be safe, I hid our pressure cooker where he probably wouldn't find it—behind the cleaning supplies. Alert for Tom! The long gasket between our two refrigerator doors easily got turned on its side. When that happened, the doors wouldn't close completely and a warning *bing, bing, bing* sounded from time to time until the gasket was repositioned. Tom added a troubleshooting page to his notebook. I told him to leave that page open because when time was up, the microwave also made a *bing, bing, bing* sound that continued off and on. The intermittent binging sounds of the refrigerator and microwave were identical. It would be Tom's challenge to identify the *bing-er*. Much like with our uninvited houseguest, a chirping cricket, it was challenging to figure out where the sound was coming from.

Tom: I'd rather look for bing-ing appliances than chirping crickets. Joan and I travelled to Vietnam a few years ago, and crickets were a delicacy there. We saw people eat them fried, seasoned with hot sauce. Yum! And as a bonus, you could floss with their crispy legs. Talk about fast food, especially when they hopped out of the frying pan! Yet, if you can remove the "Ugh" from the bug, I read that crickets provided protein, calcium and iron—just what Joan's doctor ordered. Since Joan never ate anything she swatted or stomped on, her foot probably healed slower.

Joan: I alerted Tom to a few more annoyances. If he unintentionally touched a tiny padlock icon on the stovetop, the burners would lock. When he attempted to turn on a burner, he would hear a clicking sound and see the igniter spark, but the burner wouldn't light. What good is a 20,000 BTU super burner that won't ignite? Child safety features protect children, but they probably fire up lots of adults. Our kids grew up and moved out, yet we were feeling pressure from the burners to have more!

The dishwasher has a similar *LOCK* feature, but we both learned about that from accidentally bumping against the front Touch Panel. Tom's problems could have been compounded except that he usually loads it, starts it, and they were already acquainted. Unfortunately, the operation of the only appliance he had mastered was eliminated when I bought disposable plates, cups, bowls and plastic cutlery.

Tom: If not for Joan's medical problems, I would have continued to act like a tourist in parts of our house. Many home responsibilities for too long had remained one-sided. Joan did the laundry and I wore clean clothes. Joan cooked meals and I ate half of them—not exactly teamwork. Our outdoor plants burst into color because she fed them. With what, I didn't notice. I vaguely remember her leaving the kitchen every morning with coffee grounds in her hand and coming back without them. Hey, I have weird habits too. Her indoor plants also thrived, including the orchid with fifty blooms. It all just magically happened!

TIP #8: Couples may better serve one another by not having exclusive divisions of labor in their relationship. In the past, Tom and I each handled different household tasks. During an illness or injury, life would be less stressful if each person could step smoothly into the other's role. In the future I'll look over Tom's shoulder to learn the business and financial activities he handles, and conversely continue to familiarize him with my jobs.

CHAPTER TWELVE

Get It Together

Joan: After my pre-op visit, a deluge of paperwork began:

—medical history (and parts of my geography) ✓

—a list of known allergies ✓

—a list of my medications/vitamins/herbal remedies ✓

—doctor's advice to discontinue blood thinning ✓
     agents like Coumadin, curcumin, ginger,
     fish oil, vitamin E, cinnamon, ginkgo biloba,
     and grape seed extract

—sign an Advance Directive ✓

—sign piles of forms which probably wouldn't be ✓
     read by anyone

Tom: You'd hope someone would read all your hospital forms besides hackers, yet they seem to work harder to get at them. Joan completed her plethora of papers. Then we planted a digital tree so new forms could grow and provide future patients the same meaningful writing experience. Sorry, no digital bark beetles to save you.

Joan: I already knew that the doctor's order, forbidding weight-bearing activities like standing or walking after surgery was going to be extremely limiting. At my pre-op visit, I learned about an added precaution. I was told not to leave our home for an entire month! Wow!

I realized that staying in our comfy bedroom at the far end of the house would leave me flat-out isolated. Instead I planned to recover on our den's sofa bed because of its proximity to the kitchen, a bathroom, the TV, DVD player, and stereo.

I thought about the things I needed to gather. Later I added items that might be useful after any surgery. Consult the Appendix A for my complete list.

Tom: After a quick glance at Appendix A showing all of Joan's preparations and planning, would anyone believe that same person would leap off a boulder and try to land on one foot? Had space aliens screwed up a brain probe? Our top female gymnasts couldn't stick a left-foot landing from up there, yet my wife tried it! Just proved that anyone can make a silly mistake and pay a serious price. On our next hike, should I bring a leash so she can't run loose? Or do I need a Wife Whisperer? Well, that's an issue for another day.

The job in front of me was helping to set up a new bedroom.

Joan: Tom pulled open the sofa bed, and lying at the head of the bed was an eye mask. I had left it for guests to shut out morning sunshine from a nearby skylight. I planned to use it too.

Tom: I realized that Joan's mask might also serve as a home security device, convincing any would-be burglar that someone beat him to it.

The mask's other value became apparent when the lamps went off at night. That's when our appliances, digital clocks and audio/video devices created our in-house version of a starry night. White, red, and shades of yellow and green traveled through the darkness. We saw the same colors in Alaska viewing the northern lights, but they didn't emerge as numbers, dots and streaming stereo modes. These especially lit up the kitchen and adjoining den where Joan's bed was. They also ran up the electric bill while everyone slept. Made me wonder if appliance and power companies were working together on this sneaky little money-maker.

Joan: The better part of a day was spent assembling things for the weeks after surgery. A partitioned wine crate lying sideways on my bed was for things I'd use often throughout the day. Tom helped me set up a wheeled cart and a coffee table next to my bed for my laptop, medical device and other necessaries. He connected a power strip to the wall outlet which, of course, was behind the very heavy and now fully extended sofa bed. The sheets, blanket, and hypoallergenic comforter softly poufed on the floor, and beautifully blocked Tom's crawl space. I heard muffled grumbling as he ferreted out the twisting, knotted, tangled cords and cables, and snaked the individual plugs back to the strip.

Had burnout set in? Would he want to remain my caregiver or pursue snake handling? He had always been fascinated with snakes, and they don't have troublesome feet to deal with. I wasn't venomous, so he stuck by me.

We did one more bit of prep for safety. All small rugs, runners, and any other obstructions were removed and stored out of the way.

Tom: I did like Joan's idea of picking up all our small rugs—less to vacuum. I had taken over the vacuuming several years ago after Joan hurt her back. Bending and twisting to maneuver the vacuum under furniture left her bent and twisted.

My compulsive streak actually enjoyed sucking wood floors clean. I saw the effects of my work right away, unlike being a link in a chain. Mysteries abounded when cleaning the house. Where did dustballs come from? Did teddybears shed? There were two furry ones in the bedroom. No one lived under the bed, yet more dustballs were there than anywhere! Did stuffed animals leave fuzzy droppings? Why

55

didn't Stephen Hawking ponder these mysteries? He wrote about the "The Theory of Everything"—everything except dustballs. What a waste of intellect!

Joan: I told Tom to cut himself some slack, and let the dust bunnies roll. If we viewed them as pets, they wouldn't bother us as much.

Planning ahead and taking responsibility at home were traits of my wife that I now admire. At times, though, they were irksome when I didn't have the energy or desire to do extra work at home because of long hours writing on sitcoms. It was a weird paradox—working hard for a TV family often left less time for my real one. Fortunately writing and producing led to many kinds of rewards we all shared. Those feelings and experiences primed me to now become someone Joan could depend on. Nowhere on her lists did I see that Joan planned to hire a Taster to see if her meals were safe. I'm proud of that.

CHAPTER THIRTEEN

My East Coast Cousin

Joan: Beating myself up about jumping off that boulder surfaced again. I felt stupid and had no one to blame but myself. I was zeroed in on logistics, and didn't consider the possibly of getting injured after hitting the ground from that height.

Tom: The only safe jump for Joan would've been from a similar size boulder on the moon. She would have landed only one-sixth as hard and had time for a few backflips.

Joan: If I had simply waited on the boulder, eventually Tom or someone would have come by and helped me down. Playing the damsel in distress wasn't my go-to role, so that option never occurred to me. The moral of my story—sometimes interdependence is better than independence.

The timing was coincidental when I noticed on social media that my cousin had broken her leg. We commiserated on the phone, but she saw things differently. She told me how she was walking across her den wearing comfy, contoured, healthy Birkenstock flip flops. Instead of sitting down to rearrange her toes on either side of the thong, she stood on one leg while lifting the other. She lost her balance, then twisted and broke her leg on the "one inch" fall to the floor.

She had been wearing one of the most comfortable, sensible and supportive shoes available, and still "Accidents happen," she said with a chuckle. We both laughed at the absurdity of it. That's when I wondered, why could I easily understand someone else's accident but not my own? Maybe it all came down to my mother telling me I was an *accident*. The message I took away was that accidents weren't supposed to happen. But they did and they do. At least they didn't leave the scene of the accident!

Who cared anymore, because I couldn't help laughing at someone tumbling off a Birkenstock. Boulders and Birkenstocks, who would have thought? Crazy crap just happens! I felt better. Wasn't it amazing what phoning a friend and having a glass of wine had achieved?

Tom: It's hard to feel sorry for someone who fell off a sandal. But Joan's cousin was in as much pain as anyone who had fallen from, well, two or even three inches. Joan and I pictured a scenario where the paramedics arrived in surgical masks so she couldn't see them laughing. After measuring the height of her flip flop, they ruled out altitude sickness as a cause.

They noted that Joan's cousin's eyes were clear, and no controlled substances were found in her kale chips. There was no sudden speed-up of the earth's rotation, NASA confirmed, that might have flung her off her shoes. It was just an accident ... a silly accident. When the injury occurred, and she tumbled to the floor, Joan's cousin was babysitting her grandchild. "Do it again, Grandma," yelled the toddler. "Dat was funny! Do it again!"

CHAPTER FOURTEEN

My Daughter—My Parent

Joan: I shook off the anger that had bubbled up regarding the five months of misguided and ineffective care under Dr. Two Pot-Pod. Then I had to make a clean start, but I hadn't found an easy path to enlightenment. The Dalai Lama's voicemail box was full.

As I tossed my thoughts around with my family, our daughter, Linda, offered a valuable point of view: "If Dr. Two Pot-Pod had correctly diagnosed your foot, would *he* have done the surgery? Things could have gotten even worse. And if you had been referred to an orthopedic doctor in the beginning, it may have been to someone without the communication or medical skills of the new doctor you like."

Linda was right. Despite months of pain and confusion, I may have lucked out. Dr. Five Potato trained at a top-tier medical school to become an orthopedic surgeon with an added subspecialty in foot and ankle injuries. She would be the one repairing the original injury to my foot and also what happened after that. So even after rough times, things can work out.

Instead of feeling like a victim, I felt lucky to be scheduled for surgery with a skilled surgeon, and fortunate to have my daughter's perspective to take with me into the operating room. My spirit felt lighter. It's well-documented that patients who face surgery feeling relaxed and optimistic generally do better during and after their operations.

Embrace the advice of your grown children. They're younger, perhaps more flexible in their ways and have a different perspective.

Tom: Each generation travels through adulthood with different baggage. A parent's travel bag might have a handle, with wheels that go straight ahead. Our daughter Linda's bag, however, had wheels that spin. She could change direction quickly if she saw a better path to follow. I'm glad that she was able to turn Joan's attitude around as quickly as her bag.

CHAPTER FIFTEEN

Caterpillar Crossing

Joan: Tom and I allowed additional time to arrive for my 5:30 am check-in, but we didn't check the schedule for a railroad crossing near the surgery center. As we approached, the red lights started flashing, and the barrier arm began to lower. Should we try to beat it? Never a good idea, even near a place that could stitch us back together. The arm was dropping fast, so why risk it?

Tom: Good point, and our SUV was spared a karate-chop from the rail crossing arm. I would be left driving an "S." How long could it take a train to pass anyway?

Joan: Tick tock, tick tock! Maybe because it was a densely populated area, the freight train inched past like a line of iron caterpillars. It was still dark, making it impossible to see where the train ended. After a small eternity, the caboose was finally visible. We relaxed knowing we would still be on time.

Crikey! The train came to a slow and screeching stop. The caboose was still blocking the intersection, with no platform or loading dock in sight. What was going on?

Tom: Joan reached for her phone. Maybe Siri knew of a route around the tracks. She did, but by then a line of cars had formed behind us, so we couldn't back up or go forward. We decided to let Siri go back to sleep or vent to Alexa about being rudely awakened. Artificial Intelligence girls look out for each other.

Joan: We killed time (bad word choice before surgery) guessing why the train had stopped. Did the Engineer drift back to sleep like most of us who crawl out of bed before 4 AM? Did one of the train's wheels get a flat? Obviously I wasn't fully awake when that thought occurred.

Was the train delivering medical supplies, over-priced stuffed animals for the gift shop or that delicious hospital food? Our guessing game kept us awake while we waited in darkness.

Suddenly we heard the train squeaking and slowly moving, but were dumbstruck as it moved in reverse, then stopped again—still blocking us. Why did it do that repeatedly before finally going forward like a good train?

Tom: It cleared the crossing and squealed slowly into the night.

CHAPTER SIXTEEN

They Also Serve Who Sit and Wait

Tom: No one cared that Joan was a few minutes late. But why did Joan have to be there at 5:30? Was it because doctors and nurses were at their very best at that hour? You mean they didn't wake up at four like I did, stagger into the kitchen and pour coffee on their Corn Chex?

To our surprise, there were people already in the waiting room! We sat next to a middle-aged couple. Instead of names, we found ourselves swapping details of our surgeries. He was there for a knee replacement. She already had both knees replaced, she confided in a friendly Irish accent. He said he'd been a runner since high school and all those miles caught up with him. "After I saw what a hunk he was, I caught up with him too," she laughed and winked. I asked what had happened to her knees. "It's a long story," she said casually. "I like to think of it as God's will. He showed me the way." This devout and fun lady sparked my imagination. I suddenly visualized her bouncing up and down on church kneelers, praying and singing 'til her knees wore out.

It's amazing what personal information strangers will share depending on the situation. Our Privacy Policies that day were worse than Facebook's, but they wound up helping. Sharing their injuries somehow made what Joan and her compadre-in-surgery faced seem less upsetting.

It was a small room with a flat screen high in one corner. Showing on the monitor were ducks gliding effortlessly on a tranquil pond, ringed by tall grasses swaying gently. This programming choice was obviously meant to relax arriving patients. Peaceful images, though, don't work for everybody.

When I was writing weekly TV shows, stress was a frequent writing partner. I'd often come home wound tight. What relaxed me was watching Rambo wiping out thugs, mercenaries, warlords— anyone who bothered him or other decent folk. If I were the patient, I'd rather watch a different pond where suddenly a chef with a cleaver bolts from the grasses toward the ducks. Then a flock of ninja ducks appear, who disarm the chef and dangle him from a hook in their restaurant window. Go ducks! Now that's soothing!

But I was there for Joan, not for me. It was a time for quiet encouragement and instilling confidence. I told her not to worry. Her surgery would go well, as long as Dr. Five Potato didn't forget her chainsaw. Joan told me to wait in the car.

She actually appreciated the lack of urgency. She held my hand and watched the ducks, not just to relax—she likes ducks. She had raised a few ducks when she was a kid. The ducks in the pond brought back memories. Joan's pet ducks finished her vegetables after she put them in her pocket and snuck them past her mom.

An interior door opened and Joan was led inside by a cheerful assistant, who said I could join her in a few minutes.

Joan: Sherry, the assistant, escorted me past some cubicles to an empty bed. My name was written on tape stuck to a handrail— evidence of a short-term lease. Sherry pulled the U-shaped curtain for privacy. It was a tight fit, not geared for more than one visitor unless they got in bed with me, the patient. It didn't bother me that my pre-op space was tight. Tom and I were used to flying economy.

I was handed a gown and disposable shorts. It was so chilly that I trembled as I changed quickly. What happened next was invented by some genius. A tube was attached to my gown and through a vacuum-like hose, warm air blew into the space between the cotton gown and its liner. The gown had up or down temperature controls. What a great time to be alive! Feeling snug and warm while awaiting surgery versus feeling a cool breeze whip through the back flap of a paper gown, which would you choose? The warmth totally relaxed me and no one would have to behold my goose-bumpy, jiggling body parts.

Tom: Most Americans want better healthcare. Whatever happened to the greatest healthcare ever that we were all promised? It was going to have the best coverage, lower deductibles and cheaper premiums for everyone. Our government should at least supply heated gowns to every surgical patient since all that hot air is available.

Joan: Operating rooms are kept at a low temperature to reduce bacterial growth and maintain a germ-free environment. Also the surgical team is working under hot lights while using physical strength to do their work. While the cold operating room has its benefits, it can result in shivering patients and possibly hypothermia. General anesthesia also lowers body temperature, so supplementing with a heated gown equalizes that. This gown benefited both patients and surgeons. My nurse said an anesthesiologist, Scott Augustine, MD, developed this gown. I appreciate him for keeping his patients comfortable. A gently warmed fist bump to Dr.Scott!

Before my surgery, a clipboard of official forms needed to be signed. When Sherry called me into Pre-op, I left my glasses and valuables with Tom out in the waiting room. Without my glasses, the forms were a blur. Rather than sign our house over to the hospital, I asked whether Tom could join me. I was told he refused because I was no longer naked. That sounded about right. Then in he walked smiling. He was surprised to see me in shorts. He said my legs looked hot.

Tom: Joan has nice legs. It's hardly a secret. I told her if she walked around LA in those paper shorts, there'd soon be knockoff's at Forever 51.

Joan: My vitals were taken and my IV was painlessly started on the first try. It was a good omen for the day. I can't say what, besides water, was in the IV, but thumbs up to the pharmaceutical industry. I pulled on my socks—cozy, purple skid-resistant Bair Paws, and smiled at the white sleeping bear and bear paw outlines on them. I may have shared a few words with them. Soon I'd be mock-hibernating too.

"Mom?" called a voice outside my curtain. It was our daughter, Linda, and her husband, another Tom. They had gotten up at an even more ungodly time, and had driven over an hour to give me support. It meant a lot.

Tom: Before Joan was wheeled to the operating room, I gave her a kiss and told her I loved her. The rest of us headed for the waiting room where we dug into snack bags that Joan had filled for us. We then "waited" as the sign instructed.

Joan: My mystery IV helped me to blissfully contemplate how my torn and broken foot would finally be fixed. As they wheeled me to the operating room, people scurried about preparing for the day's surgeries, but I only had to get there and my work was done—except for one thing. I needed to thank and say bye to my loyal gal pal, Liz Frank.

CHAPTER SEVENTEEN

Goodbye to Liz

Joan: Sad-I-Am. How do I say goodbye, Liz? You've been with me since birth, a true part of me. We've been on the same team my entire life and I don't like the thought of letting go of you. You were there when I zigged or zagged, stretched or lunged. Ligament Liz, you kept me balanced and did your job well on long mountain hikes, playing tennis, dancing, you name it. I worked you hard. Maybe the challenge made you stronger while you helped me have fun. We had good times together.

Is it too late to say thanks? Liz, you're partly gone already, but thank you for supporting me before my injury. And thanks especially for struggling to keep doing it, even after you were torn. I appreciate all that you did for me.

Often the quiet, dutiful, hard-working ones go unnoticed as you did, Liz, until my surgeon told me all about you. You had been silently helping me come and go without notice. But you're badly hurt now. You can no longer function and hold tight. My doctor said the few strands left of you need to be scraped off. I wanted her to fix you, join your shredded parts together, re-attach you to the bone! She said there's too much damage. It's harsh, but I'm afraid they can't save you.

I feel bad, something like when they told me they couldn't save my puppy after he was hit by a car. I wish there were something I could do for you, Liz, but I can't make you better. Now a metal plate and five screws, attached to adjoining bones, will replace you and all the work you did. It's quite a tribute that as small as you were, so much hardware is needed to handle what you alone did.

Liz never said a word. Neither did I expect her to. I was having a conversation with myself, an expression of an unfulfilled wish but also an acceptance of reality.

In my heart, I relived my decision to jump off that boulder, and the way it damaged Liz. The slow and painful delay in getting proper treatment destroyed most of what remained of her. I focused on what Maya Angelou said: "Forgive yourself for not knowing what you didn't know before you learned it." She was right.

My recently acquired body of knowledge was about more than flesh and bones. My feelings were real too. They appreciated the preciousness of life and were distressed by the loss of even a little bit of it. Feelings needed to be acknowledged and expressed because they can't be removed and replaced with machine-made plates and screws.

I told Liz I was sorry that she didn't get the help she needed sooner and would no longer be part of me—but she would no longer be in pain either.

CHAPTER EIGHTEEN

Lisfranc Fusion Surgery

Joan: I was sitting up as my bed was rolled into the Operating Room. I saw only eyes because the surgical team stood masked, gowned, gloved, and ready to begin. At first I got scared and felt like a teller during a bank robbery. But these weren't crooks. This was a different kind of operation. My surgeon had challenging work ahead of her—both brain and brawn.

My friendly anesthesiologist had called me the night before this surgery, asked about any allergies, took my history, and answered my questions. Then in the operating room, he greeted me and showed me the mask I'd wear for my anesthesia. He encouraged me to take a small breath from it, then asked me to inhale deeply as an-es—thee —zia f l o w e d t h r o o o mah m a s s s s k. I beeg an tuh z z z z z z ...

Having watched online videos, I was familiar with the procedure that would be performed. I'll spare you the tedious viewing as well as the pop-up ads and cookies on your computer. Here's what happened as I understood it. For instructional and story purposes only, so don't try this at home.

As I slept, Dr. Five Potato made her incision in a line between where my big toe and second toe attached to my midfoot. Tissue, nerve bundles, blood vessels and tendons had to be moved aside to avoid injury.

When the Lisfranc joint became visible, the remaining shreds of my Lisfranc ligament were removed. The arthritis which had formed from walking on the injury for many months also needed to be scraped off. Dr. Five Potato collected and discarded debris and other deposits using a mini ice cream scooper, heave-ho!

Tom: Out went the Flavor of the Month, Arthritis Chip!

Joan: When she finished, the arthritic bony projections were gone and the adjoining bony surfaces were smooth. With the strands of connective tissue and arthritis removed, the two neighboring bones could be joined together to grow into one. If any residual material had been unintentionally left there, it would have prevented the adjoining bones from fusing properly.

Fusing these two bones into one eliminated motion that would otherwise occur and possibly cause arthritis again. There was fairly little motion in this area to begin with. The area was designed to give feet stability and strength to support weight.

Dr. Five Potato restored the normal alignment of my foot and attached a plate and screws to maintain it. My bones were back in a position that led to stability. The doctor's fingers, like those of a pianist or string player, needed to be both strong and nimble to accomplish these tasks. Closing time! Dr. Five Potato sutured the incision.

The bunionette deformity on my little toe was then removed, an osteotomy. That means the bone was narrowed and repositioned with a screw. It was a straightforward surgery with no emotional investment on my part. It seems this was an inherited problem, but not the comfortable inheritance I would have preferred.

An X-ray machine was used in the operating room to verify that correct bone alignment had been achieved. The metal plate and five screws holding everything together were correctly placed and visible as was the screw in my little toe.

Dr. Five Potato concealed and protected my foot under thick layers of soft cotton. Having a monster scar under all that cushioning scared me. The words *scar* and *scare* are very similar, maybe for a reason. In my sleep, credits rolled and the show ended with a cliffhanger. Would my scar be ugly and frightening, or a hairline only slightly visible?

Tom: Joan's doctor was very thoughtful. She came to the waiting room in her scrubs to tell me the surgery went well and Joan should heal nicely. Obviously pleased, she gave me a copy of Joan's X-rays and showed me how she fixed Joan's foot. She functioned like a surgeon, carpenter and mechanic, seamlessly blending that trio of skills to realign Joan's bones. Impressed and grateful, I thanked her. Joan's mysterious "third ankle" was gone! And in a flash, so was her doctor. My only regret was not asking her to autograph the X-rays.

CHAPTER NINETEEN

Morning Coffee at Noon

Joan: In post-op, I vaguely heard a nurse asking me questions, but I guess I wasn't up for a chat. I ignored her and kept my eyes closed. Surgery centers are tightly scheduled so when you wake up, someone assesses you. If all is well, they help you get dressed and get out. Not so fast! Being in that cozy warm bed, still sedated and totally relaxed, was an unexpected luxury. I was in no hurry to even wake up. That killer pain, I was warned, would hit once the anesthesia and nerve block wore off.

When I checked in before surgery I was fasting, but the nurse had asked what I'd like to drink afterwards. I absolutely wanted to stay in La La Land, but I unintentionally blew my cover when she held the coffee under my nose. My eyes opened in response to the brew's aroma. My ears had not responded to her, so she moved on to see if my nose would. Nurses are a smart and clever bunch. First she wanted to know if I was having any pain. I felt some, but it wasn't bad. Like my doctor, my nurse reminded me to use pain meds right away and not wait until the pain got severe. They each said it would be hard to get it back under control if that happened. After my coffee, a few crackers and apple juice, I swallowed the pain pill.

The coffee probably emboldened me to lift the covers and glance down at my foot. Nothing scary there! Wrapped in pillowy soft cotton, it was then enclosed in a hulking cast up to my knee. It was twice the diameter of my normal foot and leg, and weighty enough to discourage unnecessary movement. My foot felt cradled in all that material, but when I tried to lift it, the cradle was mighty heavy.

Maybe the combination of pain meds and caffeine boomeranged me awake, asleep, awake, asleep. Dr. Five Potato came by and made some notes while I was still woozy. I asked how my surgery went and she said she didn't encounter anything unusual. Rather agreeably, I answered "Me neither." It was a short delirious exchange. After she left, I remembered lots of questions I had intended to ask. Nothing urgent and I'd see her in two weeks with my list in hand.

On the other side of the curtain, someone next to my bed came back from surgery in a bit of distress, so my nurse was attending to her for a while. No problem, more Zzz's for me. Despite the coffee, either the pain pill or the lingering effects of anesthesia left me woozy. In that bewildered state I wondered how robots were created. How many metal plates and screws? Liz and my bunion were gone, replaced by one plate and six screws. Was I just a little less human? Certainly more human than humanoid, but I chose to be watchful not to abduct myself. Instead I fell asleep again.

Only two people were allowed into recovery with me, so our son-in-law, Tom, remained outside in the waiting room. Husband Tom and our daughter Linda were at my bedside. Apparently I had been pulling and tugging at things before I fully woke up in post-op. Understandably they were concerned. They knew I wasn't supposed to remove my IV, so they intervened when I pulled at the tape. My bewildered brain was hearing "One of these things is not like the other, one of these things doesn't belong." Those frequently heard ear worms never quit. I was on Sesame Street telling Linda and Tom that the IV tubing didn't belong. In my world, under the influence, I was right. In their real world, so were they.

It's strange, the cycle of life. When I was first handed our newborn daughter, I studied every perfect part of her. Now this grown daughter observed and monitored me. Being a new mother had been intimidating for me, just as becoming instant caregivers after my surgery was a daunting task for my two Toms and Linda. Family members willingly took on responsibility with no preparation other than a single sheet of discharge instructions. I felt grateful having attentive and sympathetic loved ones with me.

My nurse returned, and feeling more clear-headed, I got ready to go home. This was when advance planning paid off. I arrived that morning in hiking pants. The lower portion of the leg below the knee could be detached with a zipper allowing me to convert them to shorts. Unzipping and removing one fitted leg made it easy to pull the upper part of the pants over the cast. On the good leg, I left the pant leg zipped on. The nurse helped me dress as she told me how some people arrived wearing tight jeans or leggings, but left wearing cut-offs. An aide pushed me to a waiting room where I was warmly greeted by our son-in-law, Tom. Linda, and the two Toms stayed close as I was wheeled to our car. I had been well cared for by the medical staff and by my family.

TIP #9: If you'd rather not go home in a hospital gown, wear something when you check in that you can wear again to check out. No sense trying to stretch a sweater over an arm in a big cast. Likewise, tight jeans won't fit over a leg or foot cast. Elastic waists are easy to pull on, same for slip-on shoes instead of laces.

CHAPTER TWENTY

Caregiver / Scaregiver

Tom: As I drove Joan home after her surgery, she was reasonably alert with only minor discomfort. Tom and Linda followed behind. I was determined to be a really good caregiver, but knew that my efforts were about to be put to the test.

Joan: Once discharged, you're on your own. Our neighbor had loaned us a wheelchair to transfer me from the car into our house. Our son-in-law, Tom P, was experienced with the chair's mechanics because his best friend had been in a wheelchair. Under Tom's direction, the two Toms moved me from the car, safely up the steps and onto the sofa bed in the den.

A two-part medical device was waiting for me next to my bed. One part, used to help prevent blood clots, is worn while sleeping or sedentary. I was still affected by anesthesia, coupled with a pain-killer, as I reviewed a sketchy diagram. I wrapped the cuff around my good leg and connected the hose to the machine. *Click Clack*, done. It felt like a blood pressure cuff, repeatedly compressing and releasing. I thought I was alert at that time, but later realized I had put the cuff on upside down.

Tom: Joan instinctively grabbed the cuff as she got into bed. I should have checked that she put the cuff on correctly. It was my responsibility to protect her from even upside-down clots. Fortunately we caught this mistake early on. Geez, I screwed up already! The so-called caregiver turned into a *scaregiver!*

Joan: The other section of this machine was a cooling device into which Tom placed hunks of ice and cold water. When the device was delivered the day before surgery, we had been advised to freeze containers of water so they would be ready for use after surgery. A tube circulated cold water from the machine's cooling reservoir to a balloon-like bladder buried inside my cast. It's an effective treatment for reducing pain and inflammation. Alexa, our virtual assistant, helped by giving us reminders of the on/off times.

Tom: Joan's cooling schedule was one hour on, one hour off throughout the day. My job was to keep making ice so there'd always be enough for the cooling cycles. That often required the additional freezing of up to four sandwich bags filled with water, then chopping those amoeba-like frozen chunks to fit in the reservoir around the ice blocks.

A dilemma was that the insides of the bags stuck to the ice. No problem, I thought. Just crack the ice. I'd damage our countertop if I slammed the bags on it, so I got a hammer, held a bag in one hand and whacked it. No cracks. Whacked it again. Still no cracks. Again! Meanwhile my hand got numb from the misshapen ice being pounded into my palm! *Duh!* The ice didn't have to be sterile. So I went out and dropped the bags onto the patio. Yahoo! The concrete broke the ice and I dumped it in the machine. Problem solved, frostbite averted.

Joan: I saw Tom's determination and what he was up to with the hammer. It was perplexing, sigh, murmur-murmur! Scary! If he hurt his hand, I couldn't help him and then he couldn't help me. So I suggested he run the bag under hot water to release the ice. I was annoyed that I couldn't get through to him. The solution was simple, but he had already masterminded his plan, launched his hammer, then frozen-water-ballooned the patio, all the while not even considering my suggestion from the next room.

Tom: As a Classical Latin and Greek semi-scholar, my manual work skills were limited because those skills involved knowledge a person could actually use. So I was proud of any idea I came up with —pure semi-scholar snobbery! Regretfully I didn't listen to my wife whose idea was better. Did I need a hearing aid? No, what I needed was a *Listening Aid!* It would've tuned in to my wife's practical voice, rather than the bumbling notion in my head.

Linda and Tom stayed for lunch. Joan had prepared a plate of meats and cheese along with a salad the night before. It felt good to serve Joan her first meal in bed. Handing her the lunch that she had made went well.

Joan: I didn't feel the horrible pain Dr. Five Potato had warned me about. I also didn't hate her like she said I would, not even a little bit.

Tom: On the "Screaming Infant Pain Scale," Joan said her pain was one and a half out of ten Bawling Babies—a modest pain emoji. Why not agony as predicted? A possibility involved a close friend who's a Reiki Master. The night before surgery, she gave Joan an energy-channeling treatment to promote healing called Reiki. Woo-woo stuff? I understand that energy-channeling for pain relief is a hard buy. Then again we can't see radio waves, TV signals or cell phone transmissions but they're real, and produce wondrous phenomena that we can see and hear on our devices. Who knows what other invisible energies travel past and between us?

Joan: Regardless of the Reiki, Tom was careful to follow my doctor's discharge instructions exactly. He brought me my medication, along with a full glass of water, to stay ahead of the pain the doctor had predicted. He charted the pills that first day to keep track of the time and amount. As I lay quietly in bed, my pain level was quite manageable, so after the first dose, it made sense to decline the pills. That concerned everyone around me, so I compromised and agreed to take half the dose each time. Rest in bed and drink plenty of fluids was the contradictory advice. After drinking lots of fluids, nature called and my rest was regularly interrupted. My pain level increased a bit when I moved my body, so I was glad I had taken the half-pills.

Linda and Tom then left for their long drive home, taking with them our thanks for helping, and some turkey slices for their little dog.

That afternoon as our house became quiet, I grew quite weary. Somewhere between awake and asleep, memories of a departed pet stirred me. Many years previous, on April Fools' Day, a somewhat feral cat had delivered her kitten on our back step. We named her April. Because of regular contact with her, she became tame and domesticated. When she passed on, we really missed her.

·As I rested in bed, her past visits with me seemed to be happening again. There she was staring in from outside of our sliding glass door, waiting for me to come out and hold her. When her purring stopped, she faded away.

Had I gone to her or had she come to me? Had she been there at other times when I had been too distracted to notice? Resting in bed that day, my mind was free and available. Was I on another plane of awareness or in a drugged dream? It didn't matter, April's visit gave me a lift.

At bedtime Tom gave me my last half-dose. He reminded me about the ear-splitting bicycle horn he left at my bedside in case I needed him. It wasn't the ding-a-ling type of shiny adornment. It was a silver bugle horn. Think of the resonant sound of a male elk during rutting season. When I squeezed the black rubber ball, the dual-toned, *WOOGAH-WOOGAH* would surely wake Tom, maybe some neighbors too.

When I did wake up during the night, the sedating side effects of the day's meds must have become cumulative. An enormous brain fog hung between my need to get up and my ability to get up to go to the bathroom. My thoughts had no physical backup. Drugs 1—Joan 0. I fell back asleep.

Later I drifted back to semi-consciousness, but was still in custody until drug detention let out. There was a disconnect between my body and my groggy brain, the tool used to detect pain, so there's a benefit in letting it sleep. But my bladder was wide awake and signaling! Why can't you both get along, I wondered deliriously. Strangely, my body wouldn't respond, no movement, not an inch. Got to get up, I coaxed myself.

Tom: Perhaps talking to oneself was a half-pill effect. Would answering be the effect of the other half-pill?

Joan: I struggled to think my way through the mental cobwebs, and tried to break this down into individual baby steps. Just try to sit up, I negotiated. I made an effort but failed. My uncoordinated movements were like the jerky clips shot by a first time videographer, without transitioning cross-dissolves. Eventually I was sitting upright, but still had to persuade, no, plead with each leg to move in piddling increments toward the side of the bed. Lingering anesthesia, my drug hangover and my clunky cast kept me anchored to the bed. The knee scooter adjoined my bed, but was still mental miles away.

Honking the bicycle horn just arm's length away didn't ring a bell in my loopy head and therefore not in Tom's several rooms away. I've always gone to the bathroom solo. Sounding a midnight alarm to take a tinkle wasn't my nightly habit. I should have alerted Tom, but that thought snoozed in my sleepy, drugged and vacant mind.

My medical devices had to be disconnected before I could go anywhere. *Snap, clack, yank ... Snap, clack, yank ...* sounds quick now, but it took eons to accomplish. The warning *ding, ding, ding* sounds and annoying flashing lights finally confirmed my escape.

My next maneuver involved lowering my legs from the bed to the floor. Like mindless bags of cement, they wouldn't respond. Never before had I experienced this *pseudo-paralysis.* How could I convince my legs and feet to follow through? The art of compromise turned out to be the solution. "Okay, not all the way, but a few inches over would be great." So my leg moved bit by bit, minute by minute. I baited my feet off of the bed, inching them lower onto the floor. Grabbing the handlebars, I clumsily swung my knee and cast onto the cushion of the knee scooter. The scooter's wheels weren't locked, and I was only halfway to standing on my good foot. Luckily I had a reasonable grip on the handlebars as it rolled forward and bumped into the TV stand, my first DUI. My moving violation was unpleasant, but at least I was waking up. Night school was in session. Monopod Me navigated three right angle turns, each requiring several backups and braking with my good foot, on the way to the bathroom. Thus began the adventures of *The Flamingo Kid.*

Tom: When I greeted Joan in the morning, the horn was exactly where I had left it, not a honk out of her all night. At first I thought she had slept peacefully. But her semi-stupor from pain pills was troubling. She called me "Phil." Okay, I'm kidding, but you get the idea. I checked the liquor bottles anyway! Watching her roll on her side woozily toward the edge of the bed upset me. If she were to wobble off, forgetting to disconnect her rubber tubes, I could just picture her bungeeing back into bed or worse, hurting herself. No more pain pills for Joan! I made our breakfast, checked that Joan had everything she needed, except Phil, then headed into my office feeling better when she said, "See you later, Tom."

Joan: Still groggy, I watched a little TV, but it was depressing to see multiple fires burning out of control in California. Fire fighters were having a tough time getting any of them under control. One started in a homeless encampment about 5 miles from our house. It was 100 degrees, plus the firefighters were carrying a lot of weight up steep terrain, hacking their way through the brush with axes trying to make a fire break. But roaring wind always wins in a fire, and in nearby canyons, winds blew leaves, debris and embers in all directions. The air overhead looked smokey grey, unbreathable. On TV close-ups, I could see a fire fighter's bright yellow turnout gear, goggles, helmet, face shield, boots and water hose. I drifted off to sleep for I don't know how long because time had no meaning then.

Loud noise in our back yard woke me. Out the glass sliding door, I saw the same yellow jacket, face mask, hat, boots, hose, tools and leaves still blowing wildly. Wow! The fire must have gotten out of control and burned five miles as I slept. But I didn't smell smoke. Strange! I knew we had to evacuate now as so many others already had, but I couldn't move quickly. I was scared and in trouble and yelled as loud as I could to Tom, again forgetting the horn.

Tom came quickly asking what I wanted—a drink, an apple? His total lack of concern about the fire confused me. This was a huge emergency! Alarmed and distressed, but too tired to do anything about it, I pointed, "Fire!! We have to get out of here!" Tom stared outside for a moment, furrowed his brow, then muffled his laugh as he suddenly understood my concern.

The *firefighter* was actually our hard-working gardener, wearing a yellow jacket, heavy boots, hard hat, a mask over his face, and he was waving a loud leaf blower to pile up dead leaves. Oh, it was an easy mistake, right? If I had been alone, I probably would have called 911 so they could send back-up for me and for the apparent lone firefighter out there. I'm glad Tom was with me because I'd rather write about it here than see this farcical and humiliating story on live TV. Worse would be trying to answer an overzealous news reporter's question, "Can you tell us how you feel about your house and yard *not* burning down?"

The next day, my mental clarity returned. I was able to get out of bed and coherently ride my scooter. This freed up Tom to go food shopping and do some errands. I got better at handling and parking my "self-propelled assistive device," a name no doubt created by the manufacturer to bump up the rental charge. Using my scooter, I tried to find an easier way to our nearest bathroom.

To eliminate one turn, I took a new route. Safely inside, my good foot moon-walked to the t-seat while my heavy, casted foot hung in the air. *Yowzah!* This felt like try-outs for Bathroom Olympics, but Zeus wasn't around to lend a hand.

I scootered back around two turns, then down the straightaway, parking my scooter on the other side of my bed. First I lifted my heavy cast up to the bed. I struggled to reach and Velcro my DVT cuff back on, reconnect the hoses, wrestled with twisted sheets, and finally made myself as comfortable as possible. I never heard it roll away. Floors are probably not 100% level anywhere, but we live in earthquake country where our home had been lifted and shaken several times. Things here must be a little out of kilter, but I never noticed before.

The scooter stopped with a thud against the sliding door about fifteen feet away. I turned and was surprised, but not concerned. Tom would retrieve it when he got home. After fixing lunch, he had gone out to get gas, line up at the post office, then go to the market for a take-out dinner. In bed I enjoyed the tasty fruit and veggie smoothie he had made us both, then started watching *The Shape of Water.* Later, I felt the bathroom beckon. I tried not to beckon back, but started worrying. My scooter had deserted me and the medical device company didn't provide a lasso. My crutches were standing in our entry closet because I no longer needed them, or so I thought. With my balance still iffy, I couldn't risk a one-footed moonwalk to the end of the long room to get the scooter. Nature started calling louder.

Damn that delicious smoothie! Now what?! "Go with the flow" sure wasn't the answer. Pausing *The Shape of Water* helped. I tightened my muscles and tried *mind over bladder*. Then I noticed my phone next to my pillow.

Tom: I took Joan's call while I was trying to decide whether to buy eggs from chickens that were grass-fed, grain-fed, cage-free, hormone-free, antibiotic-free or several combinations thereof, which had brown shells, white shells, yellow yolks or darker yolks in large or jumbo-size—in six, twelve or eighteen egg cartons. I was glad to rush home and help Joan go pee. I quickly put the "live and active" yogurt back in its case where it could live and be active another day, then raced the six blocks to our house. I arrived in time with Joan lying in a tight corkscrew position. I retrieved her scooter and watched her set a speed record.

TIP #10: Different models of knee scooters are available. Had I known, I would have asked for a scooter with a tighter turning radius. Then I could navigate around corners with fewer backups. Dr. Five Potato probably ordered this model because it was more stable. The hot rod models, being fast and sleek, could also tip over more easily. With either model, a parking brake would keep it from going AWOL.

CHAPTER TWENTY-ONE

Salmon or Salmonella

Tom: Joan needed nutritious meals to help recover from surgery. No problem. The first week, I mostly heated and served all the dinners she'd prepared. I'd call to Joan in the den for an occasional heating time, but being a microwave wrangler came easy. I put nothing metal inside that would cause a fireworks show, and put lids over the plates to prevent food shrapnel. Joan's reminders stuck. Even the smoke detector helped out when I—let's not go there. It looked like a new pope was elected. Serving good balanced meals was the goal. And "balanced" didn't mean I'd be spinning her plates on a stick.

Putting a dinner together myself was more challenging. Joan knew instinctively not to put a potato, corn, rice and a roll on the same plate. Good tasting, but carb overload! She told me if you're serving a potato with fish, you want to surround them with foods of different types and colors. It's a good recipe for picking dinner guests too.

Before Joan's surgery, I had jotted possible meal combinations in my notebook. To start I picked one of her favorites, baked salmon with dill. Why these two would go together escaped me. They don't hang out in the wild. But neither do turkeys and cranberries, or lambs and mint jelly. Some things you don't question. Another is that whatever you bake in the oven, you usually pre-heat to 350°. Made me wonder if Hell is pre-heated to 350 before each batch of sinners arrives! I'm guessing the dial would be turned up for some.

A key exception was salmon which should be at 400°. I remembered reading that salmon can cause a salmonella infection if it's not cooked enough. First I needed to spray the baking pan with olive oil, and be sure to brush oil on the fish. My fish didn't squeak, but I brushed oil on it anyway. Next I sprinkled crushed dill weed over the salmon—not a pretty picture, like gnats on a windshield—but the tiny dill slivers stuck. So that's why you brush oil on—it's food glue!

Into the oven went the salmon, glistening like sprinters in the first Olympics. They were also rubbed with olive oil, but without the dill. Meanwhile I had two potatoes baking in the same oven, timed to be done just after the salmon. The skin under the salmon should peel off easily like you'd expect after a 400-degree sunburn. If the skin resisted, the fish needed to bake a little longer.

When I thought it was done, I tried to flip the fish. The skin under Mr. Sockeye stuck to the pan. I had focused so much on oiling the salmon, I had forgotten to spray the pan. If the fish was cooked correctly, I rationalized, I'd have to peel off the skin anyway. Nice try, but this skin got yanked off!

Some panic set in! Was the fish cooked enough? If I cut a steak, I could tell if it was done or not, but this was an orange fish that seemed to get lighter as it baked. What's *rare, medium, well done?* I remembered Joan saying if the fish is fleshy-looking when I cut it, it needs to bake longer. I picked up a knife, made a one-inch slice and spread it apart with a fork. It was moist. I didn't think it looked raw. Cooked salmon was orange too. But in the nutty reverse world of fish, it was light enough to be well-done.

On Joan's plate was butter lettuce with grape tomatoes and honey mustard dressing, a baked potato and the gnat-speckled salmon. On mine too. After she scootered to the table, I pretended not to notice her first bite. She smiled then raved about our dinner. What a kick to have had salmon, not salmonella!

The kitchen felt warmer than usual that evening. Joan's notes didn't mention turning off the oven when the cook was finished. Hey, she's entitled to a slip-up.

As I struggled making other dinners, I was surprised by how much time it took to fix a complete meal. The meat, the veggies, the salad and the rice all had to be prepared in a certain order so they'd be ready to eat at the same time. I never realized that cooking was such a juggling act. Before Joan's injury, everything magically showed up on my plate either tender enough, juicy enough or cooked enough. After clean-up, there wasn't much time 'til I had to plan the next meal. I had no idea how hard it was to make it look easy.

Trying to make meal prep easier for me, Joan had brought in plastic silverware so there would be fewer things to clean up. But, you know, that plastic silverware looked too good to throw out. I told her that we'd use it for picnics in the Angeles Forest. So I washed and saved it, adding to my chores and the kids' inheritance.

TIP #11: Give your caregiver a break, and check out meal delivery services. Your local deli, some markets and take-out places also provide prepared food.

CHAPTER TWENTY-TWO

My Sixty-Second Bath

Joan: Soon after my injury, my right leg started aching from suddenly having to lift and carry double its accustomed weight. Muscles in my good foot—the right one—complained intensely about the balancing gymnastics required for even simple tasks like brushing my teeth. I had been encouraged to move around after surgery to prevent pneumonia and blood clots. Without an important place to go, movement that switched on pain had little appeal. Tom preferred that I stay alive, so he left little gifts around the house as an incentive for me to roam.

Tom: Surgery depletes energy, so I tried to make Joan's visits to the bathroom interesting. I asked her once to pretend she was going to the Grand Canyon, and couldn't wait to get to the rim. I had left a cookie on the rim of the tub, and a treasure map leading to another surprise, three rooms away. Something necessary and ordinary became fun, and also kept my wife moving.

Joan: Almost every behavior required rethinking. I was able to sponge bathe kinda sorta, but balancing on one weary foot at the bathroom sink for even that short amount of time became grueling. I didn't know how flamingos and cranes did it without even a vanity to lean on.

Tom: There was an expensive option. In the back of the Sunday magazine, I had seen ads for walk-in tubs. They were always next to that woman kvetching, "I've fallen and can't get up!" Since she's been lying there every week, and nobody in the tub helped her, I tuned them all out. However, a walk-in tub would need a porthole for Joan's casted foot. I guessed that feature would be as common as a porthole on a submarine. Besides, installing a walk-in tub would involve getting half your bathroom remodeled. So it would take half of forever.

Joan: Many falls take place in the shower, so if you're not feeling steady, use a shower chair for stability. It's unlikely you'll fall if you're already sitting down. For me, getting over the shower step on my scooter, or with or without crutches, and through our narrow nineteen-inch shower door opening was impossible. Preferring showers, neither of us had used our tub except to clean it once in a while. One week into recovery, a relaxing soak sounded delightful. I was pretty sure that if I first sat on the rim, I could swivel and lower myself into the tub. How to get out again using only one leg was yet to be sorted out. Tom and I would figure it out when the time came. Repeating my toe-heel-toe sidestep from the scooter got me to the edge of the tub where I sat for a minute to recharge.

Perched on the rim, I swung my good leg 180 degrees around and into the tub. *OU-OUCH!* Only one leg led the movement, but because everything was connected, the rest of me writhed in pain too. For the time being, I wished that some parts of me could divorce from other parts because of their irreconcilable differences. Impossible, so with Tom's arms locked under mine, he lowered my aching body slowly into the water. My casted leg hung outside the tub in a plastic protector. I settled in and soon *Aah! A*ll was well. As I lay quietly, nothing hurt. I told Tom he could leave, and I blissed out in my soothing bath.

Tom: I offered to bring Joan the bicycle horn to get my attention. She said, "The horn won't be necessary. I'm not taking a bath in traffic." Despite the sarcasm, it was a funny image to accompany me into my office.

Joan: When the tub was almost full, I lifted my good foot to push against the push/pull handle and shut off the water. It was odd that it resisted, again, and again. I was annoyed at how apparently weak I had become. Not only was moving my body painful, but I was getting steamed. I needed to shut off the water fast. Now more determined, I slid closer. With my arms braced on the sides of the tub I pushed my foot against the handle with all my force. *Whaaaaah!* Darn thing was jammed! I shouted, "Tom!" With my radio on, the water running and the old ceiling heater rattling, he didn't hear me.

Tom: Thus, my reason for the horn. Joan's voice is on the softer side, meaning if she were drowning ten feet from shore, the lifeguard wouldn't hear her screams. Apparently my over-sized ears were just for show, not for picking up muffled voices. On hot days I couldn't even wiggle them to keep cool.

Joan: I congratulated myself on having the smarts to open the drain and try to prevent an overflow. Still the water kept pouring in faster than it was draining. Water gurgled down the drain, but that bothered me too because we were in the middle of a drought. We had been stingy about our water use, and there it was, going down the proverbial drain. We and everyone else in Los Angeles had already gotten *shame letters* and extra charges from our Water and Power Company about perceived overuse. Could I call them hoping for a one-time exemption? I already knew the menu selection: *Temporarily disabled woman soaking in tub with a stuck faucet*, wasn't an option.

I pushed the faucet handle again and shouted more urgently, "To-o-o-ohm, Ta-a-a-ohm!" Yay, that time he heard me! Luckily he had been coming toward our bedroom to look for his glasses which he tended to misplace. Hearing my predicament, he looked as puzzled as I was. Neither of us had any plumbing skills, nor a Latin or Greek Handyman book, and this was a weekend! My first panicky instinct was to pound the handle with a hammer. I remembered the big one from Tom's frozen sandwich bag adventure. With hope and hammer in hand, Tom soon gave it a try, but the faucet stayed stuck.

Tom: What I walked in on was kind of an emergency, but I couldn't help smiling. It was like a scene from on an old *I Love Lucy* show. But back then you couldn't have shown Lucy in a tub without bubbles up to her chin. Without bubbles, my view was more interesting. Where was MacGyver when I need him? Never mind, it's my wife here. I'd have to blindfold him.

Water rose closer to the top. I knew I had to get Joan out of the tub fast! With my hands pressed around her waist, I started to lift her, but my hands slid up and her body slid down, producing a wave that rolled over the rim and broke onto the floor. Great, the tide was coming in! Grimacing, Joan flashed back on the bath oil she'd added to pamper herself—a good idea that went bad. I reached for her hands. They slipped away too. It was like trying to catch a fish with your fingers. Time was running out and water was rising! I asked Joan to move closer.

Joan: Holding my shoulders, he began turning me so my back would face him, but my left leg was still hanging over his side of the tub. Even a contortionist couldn't pull a *U-ey* like that. With water about to spill over, there was no time for discussion, but *sob, yowl*, I felt as though something might break. No time to chat! I lifted my heavy casted leg up in the air, over the water and —*G R O A N*—it swung in front of me, glancing off the wall on the other side of the tub. Why me, Lord? In that position, I understood my *scaregiver's* plan. He hooked his arms under mine and started lifting and sliding my wet, slippery body over the side.

I tried to push up with my good foot, but I panicked when it slid out from under me. Another wave washed over the side! Now the floor was oily too. We shouted anxiously back and forth. "Hold on!"... "I'm trying!"..."You're slippery!"..."Stop!"..."Don't let go!"..."*Yeow!*"...

"Hurts!" Good thing the windows were closed. With my back to Tom, and my good leg pushing against the opposite side, YOWCH! Somehow he hoisted me up onto the rim of the tub! Splash! Dribbles! *Phew,* I was out! I never even lathered up or got to lie back and relax. Sparrows take longer baths than I got! I sat—sore, frazzled and disappointed. Tom threw a towel over me, then moved right back to the still gushing faucet. A little tenderness would have been nice ... but maybe the mood wasn't right. Working furiously he unscrewed and removed the metal plate behind the faucet handle. He sprayed WD-40 everywhere, creating what looked like trickling, oily waterfalls forming multicolored designs.

Tom: Despite her pain and the imminent flood, the artist in Joan wanted me to know that these rainbow-like color patterns were caused by different angles of reflected light on the water and oil. She said the phenomenon of rainbows on an oily surface even had a name and asked if I knew what it was. "Slimy mess," I grumbled! I love the girl but I just wanted her to shut up so I could figure out what to do. After the WD-40 and a few strenuous pushes and pulls, the faucet handle started to slide on its track again.

Joan: "Thin film interference, that's what it's called."

"Fascinating," Tom said, as he pushed the handle in and the water stopped. I'm not sure he heard what I was explaining. Sadly the tiny rainbows on the faucet hardware started reminding me of my earlier waterfall and boulder blunder. I lost interest. Tom tested the faucet repeatedly and announced that it was fixed. He saved the day! My foot, then our faucet, both got repaired that week. The faucet recovered quickly, but my foot had months to go.

TIP #12: Hire a clairvoyant to tell you which plumbing fixtures are about to malfunction.

TIP #13: After surgery, consult with your doctor about taking pain meds before necessary activity. The sensory nerves in our bodies are big tattle-tales. They can transmit pain up our spinal cord to our brain in a split-second. When moving any inflamed surgical site, wouldn't you expect that the pain would be limited to that area? NO!!! It's quickly registered and felt well beyond where the surgery took place.

CHAPTER TWENTY-THREE

Casting

Joan: I slept through a lot of the first two weeks, but having to spend so much time in bed made me stir crazy. My first outing was the two-week recheck with my surgeon, Dr. Five Potato. It felt so good to roll outside into the fresh air, or whatever air LA had that day. Tom carefully guided me down our two steps on my scooter. *Wheee!* Feeling like I'd been suddenly let out of a cage, I took off like one of those joke snakes shooting out of a can.

Tom: Joan whizzed down our front path, made a quick right to my car, then honked the horn on her handlebars, nudging me to hurry up, just because. I wanted to play too. I went inside the door for Joan's crutches, and imitated her slip-sliding on them to the car. I started driving away, just because. I stopped, then backed up saying, "I knew I forgot something! Joan, have you seen my glasses? Just playin' with ya," I told her as I helped her into the car, then wrestled her "easily transportable" scooter into the back. Off we went to the doctor, which seemed to us like a mini-vacation.

Joan: Tom took a different and more scenic route to the doctor's office. Before long we were passing iconic monoliths and boulder-strewn hills in an area where Tom said many classic westerns were shot. The movie, *Fort Apache* with John Wayne, was done there as well as TV series, *The Lone Ranger, Gunsmoke* and *Westworld.* Still, I couldn't remember one western where the bad guy jumped off a boulder and suffered a Lisfranc injury.

On arrival, I quickly learned that a Disabled Person Parking Placard hanging from a car's mirror doesn't guarantee an available parking space, especially at a medical building. There are more placards than disabled parking spots, so the math is off. Luckily a regular space outside the office was open. Tom rolled into it and I rolled into the office on my scooter.

Yay, my heavy cast from the operating room would be removed! It was hard to stay happy though, when I saw how it would be done. *Eeek!* What looked like a rotating saw blade came toward me. I was told that the cast saw vibrates to break apart the cast, but wouldn't cut my skin.

Tom: What a great scene to open a movie, *The California Cast Saw Massacre!* An anxious patient is reassured by a doctor that cast removal is simple and safe, and nothing to be afraid of. She suggests, though, that it might help if the patient closes her eyes. As she does, the doctor moves the blade closer, confiding that the young woman is braver than most patients who just go to pieces. *Bwahahah! Mwuhahaha!*

Joan: I can't say I was an instant believer in the blade's benign intention. Since cast removal technology hadn't changed much in seventy years, I was relieved at not being the first patient getting this done. As the whirring blade descended, I diverted my eyes and attention—imagined instead the cotton padding going to the dump, then being carried off by birds, rabbits and mice—nature's weavers and architects. They would recycle it into soft warm nests for their young. Yep, that's what happened.

Tom: Joan's bond with nature has always given her comfort. While growing up, she liked watching and feeding animals in the park.

She retreated to her *happy place* as the spinning blade separated her cast down to where her toes were. By *were* I meant were hopefully still attached. But I couldn't see them and had no trained dog to sniff under the rubble. Then they emerged, a cute little litter of five, wiggling their way up through tangles of fibrous clumps.

Joan: X-rays were taken. Then after being snipped and pulled, my stitches were out. Only pinpoint red dots marked where they had been. My left paw was stiff, swollen and discolored ... mine for sure, but unfamiliar.

Tom: The X-ray of her left foot looked like a tray at True Value Hardware—six various sized screws and a metal plate holding key parts together. They would remain in my wife's *Frankenfoot*.

Joan: I complimented my surgeon on the delicate lines of the scars which I had feared would look grizzly. Only if you knew they were there would you spot them. In contrast, she and I both had bumpy, raised scars after skin cancer removals done by plastic surgeons. Mine was a lumpy, reddish raised scar that the plastic surgeon couldn't stop praising.

Tom: In Los Angeles the *plastic* in plastic surgeon can refer as much to the personality of the doctor as to seamless surgical results. Whether the plastic surgeon is good or not so good, you can be sure that you'll be paying a lot with plastic.

Joan: Back to my foot. The doc examined it and noticed that I felt no sensation to her touch on the big toe side. She explained that a nerve runs through the area where my Lisfranc fusion took place, and it takes awhile for the nerve to recover. Had I become aware of that numbness at home, I would have been alarmed, but Dr. Five Potato wasn't. She was satisfied with my progress, so I crossed over to the cast room for a second but lighter, fiberglass cast.

The room had seen its share of plaster, water and fiberglass before I arrived. The main attraction for me was a basket holding a selection of gorgeous colors for me to audition. The casting call began: red, yellow, blue, orange, green, black and the winner, PURPLE! The technician filled a bucket of water and dropped into it a few rolls of purple. From a big roll on the wall, he cut a length of tube-like material, a stockinette. It would slide up over my foot and leg like a second skin. He approached, holding one end of the long stockinette down at his side with the length of it dragging on the wet and dirty floor behind him. I was startled and pulled away because it would be hugging my incision. I hadn't developed an infection after surgery, and I didn't want to usher bacteria into those tiny openings where the sutures had been. Heck, I wouldn't wipe my butt with that dirty rag.

Tom: Joan wasn't afraid to call the technician's attention to something he should have known. It's uncomfortable to speak up, especially about how someone's doing his job, but it's easier than dealing with MRSA or Staph infections. He got a new stockinette to replace the one that was wiping the floor. Joan got no attitude back from her friendly but assertive request.

Joan: As much as medical care has advanced, we still need to be alert and be our own advocates. If you see something that doesn't seem right, say something politely but firmly. I did. He was momentarily taken aback, but apologized and replaced the stockinette. He wrapped the cast material until my pretty purple limb was ready for the road. Before I left I told him it felt tight. He said it should be snug in order to give my foot the support it needed. I hoped he was right, because if it were too snug, my leg might turn purple like my cast. A little girl who had a cast applied before me told her Dad her cast felt tight too. Hmmm!

What followed was a week of on and off pain where it had not been painful before. I tried elevating my foot more, and lowering my salt intake to reduce swelling, but to no avail. When I called my doctor's assistant, she immediately set me up for a new cast.

Joan: Entering the cast room this time, I felt uncomfortable. But a cheerful, new technician, Ali, greeted me with "That looks too tight!" I agreed, and thanked her for noticing. She seemed happy in her work, had a twinkle in her eye and also asked what color I liked. I still liked purple, but Ali seemed to want a challenge. "How about purple with an orange stripe?" she asked? That's another reason why I liked her.

In the early 20th century, Fauve painters represented their individual expression with energetic, bold and brilliant colors like purple and orange, and so did Ali. Horrified critics dubbed the painters *fauves* which meant "wild beasts." Every tone in artist Andre Derain's landscapes was painted with intuitive pure color, rather than painting a sky blue or a tree green.

Tom: The fauves were outstanding painters. You just wouldn't hire them as police artists. The cops would be looking for too many crooks with orange and blue complexions, violet and green hair and turquoise scars.

Joan: Since the period of Fauvism, Matisse's expressive use of color has come to be appreciated. Flat, balanced planes of color gave energy to his work. Energy was exactly what I needed. Besides, Halloween was coming so why not have fun with it. Ali removed the existing cast material with the vibrating tool, and took it all to the cast cemetery. With all the signatures and doodles on it, the old cast was its own tombstone.

Tom: Neither Joan nor I was concerned when Ali turned on her spinning blade. She was a cut-up of a different stripe, too fun-loving to be a slasher, Halloween approaching or not.

Joan: Ali returned with a brimming armload of fresh supplies: new stockinette, lots of soft cottony under-wrapping, thick cushioning pads, and the new purple and orange cast material. She was fun to be with and created a cast of distinction. It never hurt anywhere.

CHAPTER TWENTY-FOUR

Saved by the Board

Joan: I had been recovering from surgery on our den's queen-size sofa bed because of its proximity to the kitchen, a bathroom, the TV, DVD player and stereo. The bed had been used before by guests for only a few days now and then. When we bought the sofa, the bed was an afterthought. After resting and sleeping on it for a few weeks, my back was aching, even with a four-inch topper above the mattress,

Tom: We had purchased the memory foam topper for visitors we wanted to spend time with and show around Los Angeles. The topper definitely made the bed more comfortable for three or four nights. Of course living in Southern California, there were the inevitable self-invited guests spending their days at Disneyland and their nights with us. On those occasions, leaving the foam topper packed away was a thought that uh ... did occur. I was quite proud of it actually. But now I had to find a way to stop Joan's back from hurting.

Joan: Tom remembered he still had a bed board he had used years earlier. It had helped him recover from a herniated disc, but he couldn't recall where he'd stored it.

Tom: My search for the board also triggered fun memories. I found a box in the garage with my baseball glove and cap from when I pitched in Little League. In the glove's pocket was the baseball my

Dad ran down when it was fouled into the stands at a Phillies game. In my bedroom closet was another box with cards and letters that Joan and I had exchanged while dating. In there were also bogus parking tickets and notes we'd left on each other's windshields. The laughs we had shared then sure helped cushion the bumps of my teen years, a little acne included.

Where else could that board be? It wasn't under any beds. That's where we kept our dustballs and a box of extra hardwood floor planks. The search ended in the only room left unexplored—my office —where Joan was surprised I could find anything. But I had rediscovered lots of good feelings before I got there, and perhaps they guided me through the clutter. There it was—hiding behind my bookcases. I slid the board under the sofa bed mattress and soon Joan's back had the support she needed. She was *onboard* with it, so to speak, and remained in the den.

I was glad to help Joan's back, but her foot concerned me more. I worried about accidentally stepping on it when I helped her from the bed to her scooter or to the recliner. Each time I approached her, I did the ferret shuffle. Years earlier when we had pet ferrets, the little guys were often right by my feet. I would slide my feet so I wouldn't step on them. This maneuver worked with Joan too. However, when I wanted to give her a hug or especially a kiss goodnight, it felt weird … really messed with the mood. Feelings about a romantic kiss, ferrets and a very sore foot were competing for attention in my mind.

I wondered how two other lovers would have dealt with this. In the movie, *Casablanca*, the room is dark, except for reflected lights outside. Rick is playing with his pet ferrets, when there's a knock on the door. The ferrets scamper after him as he opens it. It's his former lover, Ilsa, with a cast on her foot.

She broke it jumping out of husband Victor's hotel room to be with Rick, she confesses. The ferrets are intrigued by her cast, as they crowd her feet. Rick says he bought the ferrets as comfort animals, after she dumped him in Paris. She'll never leave him again, she promises tearfully. As they move to embrace, the ferrets squeeze between them, blocking their way.

To avoid stepping on his pets or Ilsa, Rick slides his feet toward her, but the ferrets don't budge. Rick tells her to slide to the left while he slides to the right, then they could quickly slide forward and embrace. Nice try, but they can't outsmart the ferrets. Passions cool as they're repeatedly unable to connect. Rick reminds her that they'll always have Paris.

CHAPTER TWENTY-FIVE

Emotional Lows and Highs

Joan: Many people, possibly as high as 65%, will experience sadness after undergoing a surgical procedure. I was far from alone in feeling some emotional lability. Before surgery, I prepared for the practical aspects of my long recovery, but didn't anticipate emotional challenges. Feelings of loss, neediness, isolation, and thoughts about mortality all created stress. That weakens the immune system and ultimately slows recovery, so reducing emotional stress was important for healing.

There were frustrations in dealing with: periodic pain and low energy, unpleasant reactions to anesthesia and medications, limited mobility, major changes in routine, unexpected expenses, continuing anxiety about the outcome of surgery and more. Tom and I handled these temporary problems by reassessing and maintaining realistic expectations, setting positive goals and celebrating progress. The vulnerability I felt was lessened by the ongoing support of family, neighbors, and friends whose affection bolstered my well-being.

Tom: Fortunately the nasty effects of Joan's medications were short-lived, though troubling. I told her not to worry about unexpected expenses. I'd make a call and be a Calvin Klein underwear model in his next ad. She laughed, hopefully at the joke, not at the vision of me in my briefs. I assured her our insurance would cover the big stuff. Psychological stresses, however, like worrying about the outcome of her surgery, needed attention. Reassurance that she would get better and walk normally was what I kept offering. I supported her doctor's view that surgery was just the first step in a process that required healing time and physical therapy. It was not an instant cure-all, rather another painful event that allowed healing to happen. I reminded Joan to be patient because healing didn't always go smoothly. However, there were still times after a bad day or two that she'd assume that every day would be like that. She'd then worry out loud if she'd ever get better.

I had to come up with my best anti-funk thoughts about progress I was seeing. I needed to pull her up before I was pulled down.

There was one morning, though, when we were both down. Joan woke up sore and an ice pack didn't help. For breakfast, I wanted to make eggs over easy. It looked so simple when I saw a chef do it at a hotel buffet. With an egg in each hand, I cracked them on the rim of the skillet. Part of each egg flowed over the side onto the burner, while eggshells splintered on what oozed into the pan. I cussed about the mess I had to clean up. With almost perfect timing, she complained again that her foot wasn't getting better.

I lost it! I told Joan it didn't matter if she was getting better or not because an asteroid was scheduled to collide with Earth that night. She should hide in the closet so it wouldn't hit her foot. Surprisingly she laughed, though obviously not wanting to. Our tensions eased, especially mine.

I apologized for taking my botched-up breakfast out on her. Again I pointed out improvements I had seen in her condition—changes that lingering discomfort made her overlook. Our talks helped us both. Joan became more able to focus on small positive changes that were occurring. And she more readily accepted that the road to healing had occasional speed bumps, and I could get back to worrying about how long to cook chicken.

Joan: Tom gave me a gift that seemed strange at the time. A yo-yo! I stared at him, my expression resembling a question mark. He said, "It'll always bounce back. You will too. It's a good reminder."

I put the yo-yo next to my recliner and played with it when healing lagged. I wasn't good at it, except for the winding up part and trying again. For me, it didn't always bounce back like it did for comedian and musician, Tommy Smothers, and his alter ego, *Yo-Yo Man*. He worked his philosophy in a silent mystical state called *YO*. He performed, he said, like in life, somewhere between yes and no. Maybe? Watching him stringing everyone along, as well as his yo-yo, was fun. I tried to achieve my own state of *YO*. It was more like o*y* when my yo-yo didn't bounce back up.

Tom: It didn't matter. Joan's mind was gently shifted from the uncertainties of getting better to trying to accomplish something, however trivial.

Joan: I've always felt better being productive, but the leisure activities I enjoyed in the past weren't possible. Large-scale drawing and painting wouldn't work, neither would shooting and editing videos from my bed. I wasn't marketing, cooking, or gardening either. Rather than dwelling on disappointments, I needed to find a creative use of my time. Identifying negative energy was agitating and destructive, but also quantifiable. I tried but couldn't ignore it, so what could I do with it? I wanted to tackle it as a resource and assign it to a more productive job.

After a misfortune, I've often heard people say, "Everything happens for a reason," but it wasn't comforting when I couldn't figure out what the reason was. Wondering about it became a mental irritant. Then like the tiny grain of sand in an oyster, the irritant was developing into a pearl. While recapping almost a year's bizarre experiences, I realized there was enough information to fill a book. A book, great idea! Oh ... but ... I didn't know how to write a book.

Reading books was what I enjoyed. Steinbeck's classic novel, *The Grapes of Wrath* awakened compassion for the *Okies* who lost their homes in Oklahoma and migrated to California--over a million of them back in the 1930's. Their poverty and hunger felt similar to that of the homeless in Los Angeles today—things change but stay the same. LA County has around 59,000 homeless people, most of whom are in LA city. Given the plight of so many around me, I realized how fortunate I was to have time for healing, to have a home and a husband who wanted to care for me.

To keep my mind upbeat, I read the Dalai Lama and Desmond Tutu's *Book of Joy*. They acknowledge the hardships and anguish in our world. These can't be avoided but they can be turned into something productive. Desmond Tutu (2016) wrote, "If you want to be a writer, you are not going to become one by always going to the movies and eating bonbons. You have to sit down and write, which can be very frustrating, and yet without that you would not get that good result." (p.44) [1]

Bam! His words spoke to me. I should give it a try. I hired myself. My frustrations started feeling less like irritants and more like springboards. With Tom's encouragement, I tested the possibility of writing a book, first with scribbled notes. Over a few weeks, notes expanded, chapters came into existence and that's how this book started. Gradually I felt content, swaddled inside the pages of my book, a cocoon of my own making. Archbishop Tutu showed me the way.

---

[1] Dalai Lama, Desmond Tutu, The Book of Joy: Lasting Happiness in a Changing World (New York: Avery, 2016) p. 44

I noticed that Tom offered different perspectives, and often saw humor in situations not intrinsically funny to me. I asked him to come onboard, and our joint involvement became this book.

Tom: At first, I wondered what I could add to this. It was Joan's injury. It was Joan's story. However, I was with her every step of the way, except for her big one off the boulder. My life had changed as drastically as hers, just in a different way. How did that make me feel, and was I comfortable writing about it? How had I handled my sudden new roles? It became clear that Joan's injury in the forest created not one story but two, tightly intertwined. There was enough to add from my point of view, so I joined her.

Joan: We enjoyed writing together, and hoped that others in our situation might benefit from our experiences in navigating the healing process as a couple.

CHAPTER TWENTY-SIX

Visitors and Gifts

Joan: My visitors themselves were the best gifts. They brought updates, shared recent experiences and offered ideas on how to pass time—like learning a language online, binge-watching a favorite series or rediscovering the required reading that collected dust on our nightstands in high school. A few brought gifts that confounded me, especially Ellen, whom I had met in an art class a few months before my accident. I wasn't able to connect the dots when she gave me a pink and gray resizable elephant ring. The trunk cleverly wrapped all the way 'round my finger while the elephant sat joyfully on top, its tail on my knuckle. Still mystified, I was able to get out a thank you, then babbled something about it being really distinctive and, um ... er ... that it matched my pink pajamas.

Tom: There were no tusks fortunately, so if Joan scratched her nose, she wouldn't poke an eye out. Ellen said the ring was just one piece of an elephant collection she saw at the mall. "The ring must be the most popular," she enthused. "They had a whole bunch of them." Well, that's one interpretation, I thought.

"I'll bring you another piece next time I come," she promised.

"Really, you don't have to," Joan replied, somewhere between hopefully and hopelessly. But we knew the elephant ship had sailed, and would dock here again soon.

Joan: After she left, we could let loose our laughter. We tried to guess why she had chosen a pachyderm, but nothing made sense. The answer was in the "Get Well" card obscured by tissue inside the gift bag. Ellen's handwritten sentiment was simple and kind: "They say an elephant never forgets. I'll never forget a friend who could use some cheering." Oh, shame on us! I will always remember and be comforted by this kindhearted gesture.

Tom: Then there was an acquaintance that Joan knew mostly from Facebook. When she read about Joan's surgery, she had a small bouquet of roses delivered. The next morning the roses were withered and lifeless. Do I bury 'em and enrich the soil for future plants? Or toss 'em in the trash after a few comforting words? For the big questions like this, perhaps there's no simple answer, except to take my medication earlier in the day!

Joan: Next came the Marshmallow Blaster, and my visitor was thoughtful enough to bring a big bag of ammo—marshmallows to fire at will when I needed attention. This red and yellow plastic rifle was a fun gift. We all took turns shooting marshmallows around the room. Tom quickly set up some targets, one a skeevy glass vase, hand-painted with long-legged bugs. I had won it at a White Elephant holiday gift exchange and now couldn't wait to blast it. Tom stood the vase about ten feet away on a box sitting on the hard ceramic tile floor, then stepped aside. The Blaster worked like a shotgun. I loaded a marshmallow, not those sissy mini guys—the big boys. Pumping the barrel shoved the high caliber marshmallow into firing position, then after taking careful aim, *Whoosh!* I missed the vase but shot Tom in the knee. We howled as Tom sagged to the floor begging we call for an ambulance. Three marshmallows later, the disgusting bug vase was history.

Tom: If ever there was a gift to brighten one's spirits, that was it. And after we were done shooting, we could eat the ammo. I realized if Joan used the Blaster and not the horn to get my attention, I'd always be the target! Just great, a sniper on a scooter! Hey, it brought fun into the house.

Joan: Especially convenient gifts were ZAP wireless remotes by Etekcity, remote controls for any device powered by a wall outlet. From bed, I hadn't been able to reach the floor lamp's high switch. My only choice was to leave lamps *on* all night, or leave them *off* all night. With the lamp off during the night, my glue stick felt remarkably like my Chapstick—sticky situation in the middle of the night. Now just a tap on the remote and lights were on, another tap and lights went off. That made it easier to find my flashlight, which *duh* ... I no longer needed but still rummaged around for out of habit. Okay, the lights were on, but nobody was home.

During my recovery, as I moved from the sofa bed to the recliner in the den, the gift I used most was a cuddly, soft fleecy blanket that our daughter and her Tom gave me. It was a huggable blanket that brought comfort like a stuffed animal—for adults. With cooler weather approaching, the timing couldn't have been better.

Well-meaning visitors sometimes left me wondering with comments like, "You're lucky you didn't break your hip!" Okay, but being in a cast up to my knee felt like I was channeling bad juju rather than four leaf clovers! I also heard "Don't you worry, the time will pass quickly." No it didn't! Also vying for most trite words of encouragement were the classic "Before you know it, you'll be as good as new!"

Tom: NEWSFLASH: No injured or sick part of you that heals after age 35 will ever be as good as new. There's always depreciation for time and mileage. You can be better though, than the condition you were in beforehand, if you work at it. We now return to our book.

Joan: Another visitor gave me a lengthy warning about her friend who still couldn't walk or work many years after an un-named foot surgery. In addition, the foot became deformed and her friend became severely depressed. I didn't need to know that, nor could I un-hear it. Nothing to do but swerve!

We've had fun joking about get well gifts and visits, but the most meaningful gift you can receive is your friends' and family's time. Even if the visit or phone call gets a bit misguided, the visitor has given their time. It's a gift of themselves.

Tom: When you think of it that way, it's pretty special. Often the best gifts are ones you can't wrap.

Joan: While no one gave me more physical and emotional support than Tom, I felt uneasy receiving it at first. I wasn't used to having so many personal things done for me. Being needy made me uncomfortable. Growing up, I was taught the virtue of self-sufficiency and helping others, but I wasn't used to giving others the opportunity to help me. Tom reminded me that for extended periods I had cared for everyone in our family. Caring for me made him feel good, and he was glad he was given the chance. Wow! I thought my convalescence had been a burden, but to him it was an opportunity. He had gladly put his life on hold, while I had worried about losing him! I felt less of a bother. Welcoming Tom's help came easily after that. Other independent types might benefit from my awareness.

TIP #14: Be ready when friends or family ask if there is anything they can do to help. Ask them if there is something they love that they might share with you as you recover. If they are avid readers and have walls covered with books, ask them to provide a visiting library service. Someone else may love cooking and be willing to drop off a brisket one night. Maybe they could stay and have dinner with you. If anyone has a collection of comedy CDs or DVDs, ask to borrow a few at a time. Humor keeps you in stitches—the fun kind.

CHAPTER TWENTY-SEVEN

Casting Callback

Joan: I was itching to get my cast off, literally itching under it! The temptation was to slide a ruler, chopsticks or a bent coat hanger under the cast to scratch with. Never a good idea—germs, infection from scratches and death—all can interfere with the healing process. Instead, our daughter shared with me a trick you can play on your brain. I rubbed, scratched, or applied pressure to another part of my body and made-believe that was the part that itched. It created a distraction for my brain which in turn diminished the original itching. Similar things have happened when hyped stories on the news distracted readers from more important news. Shifting your attention is an often used technique.

Hey, time for my final cast to come off! The noisy vibrating tool didn't frighten me this time. Neither did the sound of the cast as it was cracked apart. Then *yech*, I suddenly saw a fuzzy, grayish, shrunken leg on the table! Oh God, where was the rest of it? Something was very wrong. What happened under my cast? Strangely, my maternal instincts momentary felt the urge to feed and nurture that skinny post of a leg, but where to put the soup?

Logic snapped back. Apparently during the long period of inactivity, my calf muscle had no work to do, so it shut down. The degree of atrophy in my leg surprised me. This lanky leg stood in contrast to the bulked-up good leg that had been working double-time on crutches and the scooter.

Tom: Atrophy like that can happen to your mind too during a long convalescence, if you don't keep your brain active. Lurking nearby for some is depression, which can make you not want to do even the things you like and can do. Joan made sure that loiterer moved on. She read books on her Kindle, had Alexa host classical and pop concerts and used her TV, iPhone and laptop to stay connected to the world and her friends. After dinner, we'd often watch movies together. Our daughter kept Joan's mind busy playing the online game, Words with Friends. If I had been laid up that long, I'd be playing Swear Words with Friends! I'd still expect to go to heaven … but probably the basement.

Joan: Very strange was the overall woolliness of my foot and leg with dead skin cells hanging on. I remembered that healthy skin constantly sloughs off dead cells. Millions of dead skin cells had accumulated under my cast until it was removed. They looked like the stuff I pull off my dryer's lint screen.

Tom: Joan's shedding continued at home, but we still let her up on the furniture. On cleaning day, I started feeling guilty about vacuuming up thousands, maybe millions of possible Joans. I sure missed an opportunity to clone her. Hey, what guy wouldn't want more than one of his dream girl? Suddenly I flashed on a vision of us on a hike. A crowd of Joans then jumped off a boulder—with more Joans waiting! Oh no, I'd have to make dinner for all of them! Serving dinner in multiple seatings would take hours. I decided to treat the Joan I had the best I could.

Joan: Even though my cast was gone, I still wasn't allowed to put any weight on my left foot. My surgeon sent me home on my scooter, again wearing that jumbo boot for protection.

Tom: Actually Joan didn't go home on her scooter. That would have involved thirty miles and two freeways without a knee scooter lane. She scooted to our parked car where a flower-bedecked crane hoisted her up on a gilded swing, then lowered her gently through the sun roof into the passenger seat of my Rolls Royce.

If only I were that rich!

Joan: At home, I thought I could make it up our front steps on one foot, using one of my crutches. I had watched YouTube videos showing how to use crutches to go up stairs. It looked more dignified than doing my bum scoot up. It involved a small leap with my good foot onto the step above. Jumping is how this whole problem started, so I shouldn't have expected a better result.

Tom took the scooter inside first, and returned with my crutch. There was no handrail. Fortunately he was holding onto me when I attempted my one crutch, one-footed jump. Staggering home dead drunk would have appeared more graceful. My crutch slid out sideways knocking over a flower pot that rolled down the step. I was on my way down too. Tom lurched forward and steadied me mid-air. No harm done, to me at least, but it was a healthy reminder of my limitations.

All bent over, Tom told me his back ached—the most horrible pain a person could possibly endure and still remain conscious. I promised to submit his name for … *uhm*, a Congressional Medal of Pain? With a rascally smile, he said he'd gut his way through it to take care of me. He suggested soaking in the tub *with me* to relieve his condition. I smiled. Taking that as a *yes*, he stood up straight as an arrow in delight! "Hey Tom, looks like you're healed!" I said, confirming my hunch. "Yeah, it's a miracle," he muttered less than enthusiastically.

That night I couldn't wait to fill the bath tub and soak my fuzzy, stuffed-animal kind of leg. I gently ran a loofah up and down my leg and de-stressed as healthy skin emerged from under what flaked off.

A loofah to remove under-eye wrinkles would be nice! My atrophied calf muscle looked spindly, like a French baguette, but felt great wallowing in water for the first time in six weeks.

Tom: Joan was able to get in and out of the tub by herself easier now, and luckily there was no YouTube video showing how to jump in and out on crutches. Without a cast, there was no need to drape that leg over the side of the tub, taking kind of a Cirque du Soleil bath while balancing on one cheek.

Joan: At home, booted up for protection, I continued using my scooter, a Jekyll and Hyde ride. Reaching to pick up something from the floor could tip the scooter sideways. Another way to keel over was when the wheels got wedged into the grout lines of our tile floor, stopping suddenly. This Boot 'n Scoot system was easier than crutches but not without its perils. A long time ago, I felt airborne on a galloping horse until it spotted a rattlesnake and stopped abruptly. My body kept moving forward but the horse's neck was there to wrap my arms around and stop my momentum. I had to be more speed conscious on my scooter. It had no neck to stop me and you can't hug a handlebar.

Tom: Joan didn't like to waste time on her three-wheeled scooter. Occasionally she'd zip around a corner on one back wheel, but when heading to the bathroom, that can be a good thing. Spaces between tiles and pointy furniture corners definitely were hazards. I guess I could've wrapped her in memory foam to protect her from accidents, but we're avoiding grout lines and end tables, not oncoming traffic.

Joan: Seven weeks after surgery, I was allowed to ditch the scooter and gradually put weight directly on my booted foot. A product called Evenup Shoe Balancer was attached to the shoe of my good foot. It added one half to one inch of height to offset the extra height of the boot. The first day I was able to walk about twenty-five feet with hardly any pain. Great, I thought, my foot feels almost normal! However, as the distance increased, so did the pain. What was happening? I was supposed to be getting better! That's when I learned from Dr. Five Potato that the complete recovery would take nine months! Might as well have had a baby too!

At our first visit Tom and I remembered hearing about the two-month post-op no weight-bearing rule. We may have blocked out everything after getting that jolt. It didn't matter. The surgery needed to be done, and she did it. The healing needed to be done, and it was my body's job to do it.

Strengthening those 100 muscles, tendons and ligaments and learning to walk painlessly, with a metal plate and six screws in my foot was my new challenge. How could I do that? My foot's muscles had atrophied. I gathered bits of information from several websites and devised a method that made sense to me. I rested my injured foot on a scale, and pushed down enough to get the scale to read 25% of my total weight. I paid attention to that feeling. That was how much pressure I put on my foot the first week, using crutches to support the rest. In the beginning, 25% felt like quite a load. After about a week, I stepped on the scale again, and 50% was my new goal. In consecutive weeks, the percentage went up and my foot got stronger.

Feel-good moments came when I was first able to venture outside in my walking boot and crutch. A woman exited from one of a long row of exit doors, walked straight over to where I was headed, and without a word, without even looking my way, opened the door so I could enter. It took her 30 seconds, but her kindness was timeless and heart-warming. Thinking about her comforted me then, still does.

More than once, people stepped aside to let me pass first in narrow store aisles. As I cautiously navigated through Target in a motorized cart for the first time, bad childhood memories surfaced about amusement parks' bumper cars that never seemed to respond as expected. Back then, bumping into someone else for fun was actually encouraged, but at Target, I worried about a customer becoming a target. Another shopper must have noticed the unsure look on my face. She gave me some love as she stepped aside. She cheered me on and told me I was doing fine. None of it made news, but human beings who didn't know me, did the most caring things. These experiences restored my faith in the kindness of strangers. That take-away was priceless, and I didn't even need a store coupon.

Soon after, I was allowed to start driving, but my car battery was in worse condition than I was. I was recovering, but the battery was dead. I knew AAA would charge or replace it, but Tom didn't call them. He continued driving me wherever I needed to go. It took a while before I realized he was concerned about my being out on my own two—correction—one good foot. The dead battery stayed dead until I was back to normal. Did I mention how much I love Tom? A lot!

Tom: That love began when Joan was fifteen, I was seventeen, and we started dating.

CHAPTER-TWENTY-EIGHT

Mortified

Joan: I developed more strength and mobility and was looking forward to getting back to our bedroom at night. During the day, I would still use the recliner in the den to recharge after giving Tom a hand in the kitchen. Between meals, Tom helped transform my infirmary back to a den.

Tom: I threw all the bedding except the pillows into the washing machine. A few tart cherries and three salted pistachios had escaped from Joan's snack bags and had been hiding in the sheets. I tossed them in the yard and made a squirrel happy.

Joan put away her ice packs, massage roller, thermometer, pain pills, laptop and Kindle. I offered to put back all her other stuff. But where does a guy put his wife's gum picks, Q-tips, emery board, cuticle scissors, lip gloss, blush, eyebrow pencil, electric shaver and battery-powered mirror? On her bathroom's two wall shelves with the eye cream, moisturizers, lavender massage oil, ring holder and portable radio? The shelves might collapse. Under the sink with the 409, extra soap, shampoo, conditioner, mouthwash and heating pad? Seemed odd. How about the medicine cabinet? When I opened it, a box of Band-Aids and Polysporin fell out. No Vacancy! The vanity was crowded already, but I made room for her hairdryer and electric toothbrush. Aha, the mirrored wall cabinet! There was space there for maybe another Q-tip. Joan's things should come with GPS!

Where should I put the Fast Drying Sculpting Spray, Color Repair Triple Rescue Spray, Extra Hold Humidity-Resistant Touchable Hair Spray, and the demanding Seize-The-Moment Freezing Spray? Not to mention the volumizing brushes, barrel brushes, natural boar bristle brushes, detangling and rat-tailed thin-toothed combs! At least it explained why Joan never had *bed-head* in the morning!

The stress of where to put my wife's things was too much, so I dumped them all in her giant empty boot box and left it on her bathroom floor. A little mystery in our relationship was okay.

Joan: The pillows and bed linens were stored in a wooden chest which served as a coffee table in front of the recliner and couch. It sounded like the blow of a whale as I pushed the pillows and bedding down hard in order to close and latch the top. That whale's not getting out of there!

It was a big job that morning, but finally all that was left was for the bed to become a couch, and my sickbay to become a den again. Tom lifted the foam mattress topper, rolled it tight and tied it until it formed a snail at each end. This snail didn't slither into the closet on its own, so that was one more job for him. Then the mattress and metal bed supports could be folded and slid back beneath where the seat cushions would go. Tom lifted the foot of the queen-sized bed and pushed forward. It didn't move. I encouraged him to push harder. No luck that time either. I asked him if he really pushed harder because nothing changed. Looking miffed, he said he did.

I had easily opened and closed this bed for guests many times, and couldn't understand why it was so difficult for Tom. I urged him to give it one more try. *Sheesh!* Sometimes it's easier to do things yourself than to explain them to someone else.

Tom: I was starting to sweat and feel less than adequate. I braced myself, then gave it my best push yet!

Joan: Tom grumbled when it still didn't budge.

Tom: Why do words with only four letters come to mind when you're frustrated or angry? Because you can say more of them in less time? Being somewhat emotionally repressed, I blurted out just one, describing something men and women like to do together. Joan laughed and mimicked my quiet and controlled blurt, then went on a fun run of her own.

Joan: The byplay eased the tension, but I was still confused. I would have noticed if something had snapped or had broken while I was using the bed. I asked Tom, if it wasn't broken, why couldn't he slide it back in place?

Tom: With no logical answer, only one thought came to mind. I didn't like it, I told Joan. I needed some T-Boost for Men to bump up my testosterone. Obviously I had sprung a leak.

Joan: I realized my question wasn't the most tactful. I felt like my mind was unraveling. My directions about how to close the bed were bunk, I said. I tried to recall what else I might have done, but drew a blank. I felt like my memory had been erased, I confessed, and that scared me.

Tom: "Welcome to the club, whatever your name is," he said with a smile.

Joan: I quickly brainstormed, hoping for at least a brain shower. Maybe Tom needed to lift the mattress and bed frame higher before pushing down and folding them under. Surprisingly he thought it was worth a try. He hoisted the frame much higher than I ever could have, then pushed down and forward with all of his might. By now beads of sweat rolled down his face, but the bed wouldn't fold or slide back where it belonged.

Tom: "How about if we torch it? I'll bring in the hose so nothing else burns."

Joan: He said it so casually, I hoped he was joking. Meanwhile our situation had worsened—the mattress and frame wouldn't lower back down. With the *queen* partly inverted in mid-air, some black legs were outstretched pointing toward the ceiling, and others at the opposite wall. I said it looked like the dying contortions of an enormous bug after a blast of Raid. *Aaagh!*

Tom: It was the biggest bedbug you could imagine.

Joan: Totally frustrated, Tom wanted to trash our sofa bug. Another challenge—how could we get it out the door? Neither of us felt up to the task of unscrewing the sections piece by piece. Discouraged but still determined, Tom gave it one more round. Like an angry pit bull, he yanked it sideways, shoved it left and right, shook up and down on the airborne mattress and frame until ... freaky, a few inches of something stiff and flat stuck out the side. What got busted in his jerking slam-bam-bam?

Slowly a puzzled recognition of something vaguely familiar evolved. As my awareness of what it might have been kicked in, my mouth dropped open and wide-eyed embarrassment flooded over me. Our eyes met. I tried to read Tom's expression. Had he seen it? Did he yet know what I suddenly suspected? *Uh oh, w*ould he be relieved, surprised, angry? Was that when he would walk out totally humiliated, frustrated and slam the door behind him? My thoughts jumped around as Tom's face changed expression. After a moment, we looked at each other and exploded in laughter, realizing simultaneously that it was the weapons-grade fabricated wooden bed board! Strong sucker! We walked around the side and yanked it out!

Tom: Joan and I learned a lesson that day not taught in schools —wood doesn't fold. Not fabricated wood. Not even rubber trees.

Joan: Closing the folding bed and moving back to our bedroom were milestones needing to be celebrated. Even if you're in a body cast up to your chin, you can still enjoy a little champagne through a straw or a sweet treat as you recover. Frozen yogurt was my *mouthgasm* for each accomplishment.

Tom: After our yogurt, we enjoyed my suggestion for celebrating too.

CHAPTER TWENTY-NINE

Physical Therapy — Round Two

Joan: Physical therapists are unsung heroes in the medical world. After earning a Bachelor's degree, a three-year program is required for a Doctoral Degree in Physical Therapy. Simply put, they show people how to manage and improve their conditions. They have many modalities to work with: stretching or strengthening exercises, encouragement, balance and gait training, encouragement, electrical stimulation, encouragement, massage, encouragement, and ultrasound.

Tom: Why so much encouragement? During her previous round of physical therapy, Joan got some in-office treatments during each visit. Additional benefits, however, resulted from doing exercises at home that her therapist had taught her to do. She needed to take the therapist's encouragement home along with the exercises. Healing was partly up to her.

Joan: After injuries, most parts of the body can regain strength gradually. However after surgery, my foot had to suddenly support my entire weight. The problem was that my strength and range of motion had become seriously limited. I wasn't happy about being weak and having a lot of work ahead. I griped to Tom as we got in the car to go to PT.

Tom: I reminded Joan that if she were a horse in the old west, she'd be shot. If she were a race horse with a bad leg, she'd be put down with a needle. No cast, no physical therapy, no encouragement. Just a bunch of bettors angry that she didn't finish in the money. Her rare display of self-pity faded.

Joan: An order from my surgeon had set me up for an assessment with Lea, the physical therapist who had time available. After an assessment, she recommended Pool Therapy as well as some exercises on land later. She explained that the pool water would partially support my weight. My foot would strengthen gradually without my full weight pressing down on it right away.

Our Health Center treats people who work in the entertainment industry along with their families. An incredible Aquatic Pavilion was funded by Jodie Foster. It was a generous gift that has helped many. I understood the pool's benefit, and swimming had always been fun, but I was unsteady. With one good foot, a boot on the other, and a crutch for support, I was concerned about a slip and fall on the wet tile floor around the pool. Lea nixed my worry. With full assurance that she wouldn't let that happen, she asked me to bring a swimsuit and water shoes to my next appointment.

Tom: This was legitimate physical therapy, not some show biz version of it. Still I couldn't help getting this image in my mind of actresses in water shoes with five-inch heels. I love poking fun at our business, but we can only point with pride at Jodie Foster.

Joan: Lea saw the struggle I had with walking. To replace my clumsy crutch, she suggested I buy a cane instead. Tom still drove me everywhere, so we stopped at Walmart on the way home from therapy. "Always Low Prices!" No surprise that I found an adjustable cane with a padded handle for only sixteen dollars. As we were leaving, I was tempted to have some fun. I could prop my no longer needed crutch against the Assistive Devices aisle with an attached note, "MIRACLE CURE AT WALMART!" Being first to post the image on social media would have created an urban myth and also prompted pilgrimages to Walmart. Their parking lot was jammed already, so I decided to donate both crutches to charity. Let them help somebody else.

At my next PT appointment, as I entered I was in awe of the brightly lit, sparkling indoor pool. The California blue sky, trees and flowers were visible through huge commercial-size windows surrounding the pool. They brought the outdoors in. Music played as Lea asked me to have a seat in their PVC wheelchair. I left my boot and cane poolside. Lea wheeled me down a long ramp into the heated water for therapy. When our daughter was a child, she played with her Barbie in a large Barbie Dream Pool. Now I felt like I was Barbie, except my waist wasn't a three.

Lea parked the wheelchair in its designated spot at the bottom of the ramp in the corner of the pool. I had a personal pool valet. The buoyancy of the water supported me as I stood up on both legs—no boot, no cane, no crutch—for the first time in months. Lea also fastened a flotation vest around me, so even more of my weight was supported as I walked around the pool, forward, backward, and sideways. Then while I was holding onto the bar on the side of the pool, Lea asked me to do range of motion exercises against the resistance of the water. A half hour zipped by and all too soon I was back in the wheelchair. Lea must have felt the burn as she pushed hard to roll me back up that pool ramp. That day, I knew my therapist worked harder than I did.

I couldn't take the indoor pool home, but I was given homework. Lea asked me to ice my foot twice a day after doing my exercises. Initially I used gel packs which were tricky to balance on my foot. Also, depressions in my foot never got cold enough while bony protrusions got too cold. Per Lea's suggestion, Tom filled a rectangular container with cold water and I plopped my foot into it. He then added a few large blocks of ice. The floating icebergs gradually lowered the temperature, and my entire foot benefitted equally. Afterwards my foot felt better. Lea said it helps, but not everyone can tolerate the icy cold.

Tom: Joan could. Was she part polar bear? A few years back we took a winter vacation at Chena Hot Springs, sixty miles northeast of Fairbanks, Alaska, so Joan could shoot photos of the northern lights. On our third night there at two a.m., with green curtains of light dancing in the sky, the thermometer hit minus thirty-eight degrees Fahrenheit. Yep, thirty-eight below! I was wearing thermals, two pairs of pants, a sweater, two coats, a wool scarf, a fur hat pulled over my ears, snow boots, two pairs of socks and gloves. I looked like an igloo with legs. Several feet away was Joan, barehanded, gleefully adjusting her tripod and lenses and shooting different exposures. She did this for hours, occasionally putting her hands in her pockets. If I didn't know her, I would have guessed that inside her boots were white furry paws. I asked Joan if she was a shape-shifter.

Joan: I was simply a woman determined to get better. With exercise and pool therapy, I noticed improvements. The numbness at the base of my big toe regained sensation, as Dr. Five Potato had said it would. Some exercises involved small, controlled movements so I didn't anticipate the substantial effect they would have. Not only did my range of motion increase, but my discomfort decreased. I started therapy with one leg atrophied, but in little more than a month, my shrunken calf muscle rebounded to almost its original size, and I was back in athletic shoes.

Some friends commented that their physical therapists were like drill sergeants giving orders. Maybe that's true for certain conditions, but Lea was supportive and encouraging. In fact, the very moment an exercise hurt, I was told emphatically to stop doing it. I was allowed to revisit the movement that caused pain down the line, but not as long as it hurt.

Lea's keen observation detected whether individual muscles were activating or not, despite clothing that sometimes obscured them. She helped me identify and switch on the slackers. Strangely, Lea read my body better than I could. My sluggish muscles had their escapist moments, but before long they were back at work. Lea and the entire PT team got me back on my paws—oops, I meant feet.

TIP #15: Here's a way to secure an ice pack to your foot using an orthopedic adjustable boot. Wear a sock, and drop your foot into the opened boot. Place a cold gel pack over your incision. Then loosely velcro the sides of the boot together. If your foot feels uncomfortably cold, wear a thicker sock. The boot will hold the icepack in place so you can elevate your foot for fifteen or twenty minutes.

CHAPTER THIRTY

Six-Month Checkup

Joan: X-rays showed normal healing of the bones that were fusing together, but why was I still experiencing pain with certain movements and moderate walks? My surgeon said some people have problems with the metal hardware. She explained that she could remove the metal plate and screws one year after surgery when healing would be complete. At that point they would no longer be necessary. However, if there was no problem at that time, the plate and screws would be left in place. That's what I had hoped would happen.

The laces of my shoe crossed directly over my incision and hardware. To reduce pain, Dr. Five Potato suggested a clever way of lacing up. She told me to start at the bottom with the normal crisscross pattern. Over the scar, thread the laces straight up from eyelet to eyelet along the sides to eliminate pressure over the incision. Then finish with the crisscross pattern closer to the top. Check online for variations of lacing patterns for different conditions, or just for fun.

Tom: Dr. Five Potato's suggestion was ingenious! Did she learn that in med school, or as a Girl Scout winning merit badges for knot-tying and lacing? Her simple solution greatly eased Joan's discomfort.

Joan: Full recovery would take some time, but meanwhile I often glanced out my sliding glass door at the garden I've loved and tended for many years. I was familiar with how my varied plants performed through the four seasons. Yes, we do have seasons in California.

One plant in particular has provided much pleasure. This azalea reliably budded out several times a year, unlike more stingy once-a-year bloomers. It has given me large carnation-size pink and white blooms, but with rippled and striated petals like typical azaleas. This year it started flowering when I came home from surgery, and continued blooming seven months along in my recovery. Why so continuously and why during fall and winter months? I believe it was a cheery Get Well gift, the yard work of the *Master Gardener*.

I started looking ahead to when we could return to Rose Valley Falls and see what we missed. Foiled again! There had been fires in Ojai, and the trail was closed. Apparently some scofflaws ignored the signs and continued hiking in, hanging out, and leaving lots of litter behind. By the time the trail reopened, the waterfalls were reported to be trickles. We hoped the next winter's rain would restore the falls.

Tom: During the California winter, people also hope that it doesn't rain too much. Several days of rain sometimes resulted in rocks and debris being washed down from higher elevations, blocking trails, streets and causing flooding. Torrential rains in canyon areas can also trigger mudflows, sweeping away cars and anything in their path. Who could ever imagine that a solidly built house could suddenly become a mobile home?

Joan: However, when winter rain is moderate, nothing is more beautiful than trails lined with wildflowers, hillsides ablaze in color and waterfalls creating misty rainbows. It's nature at its very best—giving, not taking.

CHAPTER THIRTY-ONE

One-Year Checkup

Joan: In most doctors' waiting rooms, you have no idea what's wrong with everyone else, and no one is so inappropriate as to ask about another's malady. Injuries in the orthopedic waiting room were so apparent that they spoke for themselves. There was no hiding a large cast or medical device. Patients with good legs deputized themselves to assist someone with a fractured leg needing to pick something up. Appreciative conversations then began naturally.

Across from me a fit, spandex-clad young woman was straining to elevate her casted foot on another chair that, with help, she pulled closer. There must be an interesting back story I thought.

She told me that she fell while mountain climbing in Patagonia, not the store, but a picturesque part of southern Argentina near the Andes Mountains. She was evacuated, X-rayed and had a cast applied to her broken leg. She said she was also given pain medication, but her active vacation was over. The pain meds helped but made her heavy-headed, actually lead-headed. She was able to book a flight home to Los Angeles leaving early the next morning. Taking more medication that night would have eased the pain, but she was concerned about oversleeping, balancing on crutches and being denied boarding if she wobbled or stumbled toward the gate.

Safely aboard, she could pop a pill and hope for relief. Instead, on the long flight home, her leg throbbed more. Probably her leg continued to swell, but her fiberglass cast wouldn't expand. Maybe it was applied too tightly right from the start. Sounded familiar, but when it happened to me, I wasn't on a 6,100 mile flight home from another continent. The fracture was bad enough. Yet it was no surprise when later she learned that she developed a blood clot from the tight cast in a tight economy seat.

Tom: Apparently no one with the airline was humane enough to upgrade her to a non-clotting seat. She obviously needed a seat with actual leg room because humans don't fold their legs under like birds. Did they think the woman's cast and crutches were a ruse? Certain practices make no sense. Airlines tend to put entire families in spacious bulkhead rows, even though parents can't keep the kids in their seats. I've never heard of a toddler getting a blood clot. Heck, I bet little kids would rather be up in the overhead bin throwing blankets and pillows down on everybody.

Joan: We've all had to endure unpleasant flights, so all of us in the waiting room were happy to see Patagonia Patty taken quickly. She needed to have her tight cast removed and a new one put on. Every one of us sympathized with her, and felt we were the lucky ones.

An elderly man arrived with his left arm in a cast. Uh-huh, he was left-handed. The right-handed scribbles on the forms he filled out made that clear, as well as unclear to read. His story started with him on his roof. Many would wonder why he was up there in the first place. Oh, we've all been there. Not actually on the roof like him, with his arm wedged in the rain gutter after he slipped, but doing something outside of our skill set to save time and money. Subtract the time saved from the healing time ahead, and he'll be behind about two months. As far as money saved? None! Instead, the run-up in medical charges and physical therapy could have made a sizable deposit on a new roof and gutter.

Tom: A millennial fellow entered from the examining rooms section with casts on each thumb. He seemed surprisingly upbeat so I asked if he had been thumbing rides too vigorously. He said his electric can opener got stuck. So he tried to push open the slippery lid of his soup can with his thumbs, and sliced his ligaments. He said he was fed up with cooking. Maybe next time a meal less complicated?

Joan: More patients joined in about their accidents. Fractures weren't planned so people's brains were still trying to grasp and integrate what had suddenly happened to them. It seemed that talking about their mishaps helped people process them. Maybe retelling a traumatic story helped a person's brain find a place to store something that made absolutely no sense. The waiting room exchanges became baby steps toward recovery.

My pain had lessened over the months, but at this one-year appointment, the amount of comfortable walking I could do still had limits. I could accept my limitation as my new normal. Or after talking with my surgeon, I could accept her offer to remove the hardware. Another surgery, despite less pain and a shorter recovery, wasn't what I wanted. It was what I needed.

Throughout my life I've found peace and serenity while walking in forests or country trails, and there are more national parks I'd like to visit. So a second surgery was my logical choice. A referral was submitted, pre-op physical was done, prescriptions were filled, my home recovery area was once again stocked with everything I would need, starting fortunately with Tom.

Tom: How 'bout that, another surgery! We had hoped the initial surgery would be the answer. It was partially, but all agreed that a follow-up was needed. Former New York Yankee great, Yogi Berra, said it best: "It's deja vu all over again."

CHAPTER THIRTY-TWO

Coming Unscrewed

Joan: For this hardware removal, Tom and I were glad to have been assigned a later arrival time. Drats on needing a second surgery, but equally unnerving was entering a totally empty waiting room. Nobody there! The year before the room buzzed as patients shared their experiences and eased each other's jitters. Despite careful planning, I must have come on the wrong date! Totally flustered, I sat down to scan my paperwork just as a receptionist walked around from the back saying, "Hi, Joan." Wow! I had been there only once before, an entire year earlier. I felt like a celebrity on a reality surgery show."

As it turned out, my name was no mystery to him because everyone else had checked in, and I was the last patient on the list for surgery. *Aaah*, things were making more sense. I followed a nurse to a long room with mostly empty beds lined up on either side. Only a couple of post-op patients were there recovering quietly, compared to a full house last year. What happened to all the rest of them, I worried! I approached the charge nurse's desk anxiously and asked why most of the beds were empty. Unconcerned, she shrugged saying there was a convention for orthopedic doctors somewhere, and many were out of town. Ohhhh, perfect timing! The room was peaceful and finally so was I.

Same drill as the first time: change into a gown, vital signs, answer questions, sign forms, and wait with Tom. Walking past my cubicle several times was the caring and light-hearted anesthesiologist who had prepared me for my first surgery. I was happy and relieved to see him. He looked at my bedside chart and then at me. I said it was nice to see him again. I probably wasn't supposed to notice the handfuls of supplies he was concealing in his fists and his bulging pockets.

He pulled up a chair and said, "Can you believe just yesterday I was in charge of trash collection? This is my first day working with patients, but they say I'm catching on really fast." Playing along, I told him it was great to hear they were promoting from within, so that everyone at the Surgery Center had a chance to advance.

We also commiserated about the high cost of black-out drapes, a necessity for people like anesthesiologists who are in bed long before dark in order to rise by four a.m. I was redecorating a bedroom so his experience of ordering drapes online was bonus information. More teasing, a few casual arm squeezes, and my IV was somehow started. He was good! Much of what had earlier been stashed in his fists and pockets was now securely attached to my arm. The torn paper wrappings and cotton balls were scattered on my bed. He mentioned that another anesthesiologist would be with me in surgery. I was sorry to see him leave so quickly ... but reminded him to collect the trash he left on my bed.

My surgeon was finishing a surgery and I would be next. My gown was again attached to the adjustable warm air blower, and it was impossible not to relax in that spa-like coziness.

Tom: Joan and I felt there was less to worry about this time. The same surgeon who put in the plate and screws would remove them.

She knew Joan's foot inside and out, you might say. Even so, we were told hardware removal wasn't a simple surgery. During the year, tissue and bone had grown around the various metal pieces. Care was needed because of the risk of infection, hardware breakage and possible nerve injury, but we were confident in Dr. Five Potato's skill.

Our insurance gave us no worries either. Fortunately we didn't have one of the government's short-term medical plans, where the only pre-existing condition allowed is health. Something like hardware removal would probably never be covered because having had hardware installed would be considered pre-existing.

Joan: It was time. Tom and I hugged and reminded each other that after eighteen months of medical treatments and procedures, our lives would soon return to normal. It was a nice thought to hold onto as I was wheeled to the OR.

Once inside, my foot was positioned and propped at the end of a narrow table. Everyone was masked and ready. I was in mid-sentence asking a nurse where my doctor was when a soft, nasal mask was dropped over my nose from behind. No hello, no words of encouragement? I already knew that arm and body restraints were used during surgery, so patients wouldn't move at critical moments. Regardless, they should have waited 'til I was asleep before fastening them. I had no plans to escape, but being tied down by strangers was disturbing. This was an operating room, not a Quentin Tarantino film! No matter, lights out, I was gone! Many nights at home in bed, I longed for that instant transition to sleep, but without being bound first.

All too soon, I woke up groggy with a nurse asking if I had any pain. Why, I slurred, *ya wan sum?* She patted my hand and gave me Percocet, a one-time dose to head off any pain. Then Tom was called to be with me. The comfort in having my other half right there was beyond measure. Also I knew he carried a credit card-sized multi-tool in his wallet, so he'd cut me free if they tied me down again.

Tom: It had a sharp blade and five other tools, but its best feature was that I could open it, unlike a certain Swiss knife.

Joan: I had been asked before surgery whether I would like to keep the hardware they would be removing. *Yech*, that's not something I'm asked everyday. Momentarily I pictured it all fleshy and bloody, but then, well, you never know when you'll need a few good screws. I finally got to see the culprits that had been hurting me. There they were, scrubbed clean and handed to me in a sterile plastic bag. One of the screws was over an inch and a half long, so how could it not hurt? The cluster of shorter screws rolled around the metal plate, resembling game pieces in the old *ball in the hole* game.

Tom: I've read about surgeons using hardware to repair athletes' injuries, but I had only seen those surgeries done by veterinarians on TV shows. A vet drew a picture of where, say, a dog's bones were broken, then marked where hardware would join Spot's pieces back together. It all became real when a Black & Decker drill-driver burrowed through bone, metal pins were inserted, wires twisted and screws tightened. Then weeks later we saw Spot throw down his crutches and chase happily after a stick.

Joan decided to keep her hardware. It was admittedly a curiosity. Showing your body hardware at a party might be a good conversation starter, but so would saying hello and your name. That little bag of metal was a tangible reminder of what helped heal her foot despite its annoyances.

Joan: My doctor said I could wear my boot and walk after this surgery. I wanted to play it safe the first week and used my scooter. It took me everywhere I needed to go. My walking boot made a reappearance until the swelling subsided enough to slide my foot into a regular shoe.

Tom: Actually Joan might have been able to slide her foot AND shoe into that boot, with room for a nursery rhyme family too.

Joan: Our recliner was comfy while elevating my foot above my heart as I had been instructed. However, one time when I reached for a cup on the coffee table in front of the recliner, I didn't lower the leg rest first. Because I couldn't do my usual yoga, I saw it as an opportunity to lean and stretch forward. *Seated forward bend* is the yoga stretch that supposedly induces relaxation and relieves stress. Not that time! My recliner suddenly revealed its dark side. The forward shift of my center of gravity, pressing down onto the leg rest, lifted the chair's back legs into the air while tipping the footrest down 'til it hit the floor. *Plop!* My recliner became a sliding board and down I went! *Whaaa! Yikes,* dumped by my favorite chair! Sliding two feet down onto my butt didn't break any bones, but it earned me a new nickname from Tom—"Your Heinie-ness!"

My foot's weakness from inactivity was short-lived, thanks to the same exercises I had done after the first surgery. I was noticing improvement on an almost daily basis.

Tom: Joan's foot obviously was getting stronger from her daily exercise program. She was in no hurry, however, to do anything strenuous, like chasing after a stick. That's what she had me for, she said with a wink.

Joan: The azalea plant outside my glass door bloomed again like a lover's serenade in the open air. I had been unable to provide it with any care except water over the past year. Tom filled in for me with a few feedings, and it put on another drop-dead, gorgeous show.

Last summer, I learned that I could take a cutting from it and start another plant. Mother and baby did well. In its tiny pot, baby azalea grew only a few leaves before a flower opened. Like mother, like child.

CHAPTER THIRTY-THREE

Takeaways

Joan: Walking became less painful as my incision healed. Doctors Four and Five Potato each made the right decision to do the original Lisfranc and bunion surgeries, followed by hardware removal a year later. A bonus was that I could wear the dozen pairs of shoes that I had stopped wearing shortly after buying them. My irritated bunion had rejected them all after only a few weeks of use. Following surgery, both my feet and my wallet were happy with the practically new shoes in my closet. It's been nearly two years since my initial injury, but all that time wasn't wasted.

Besides the fusion of bones in my foot, as important was the cognitive fusion of positive thoughts and behaviors during this experience. I remember how vulnerable I felt on crutches, trying to move quickly without skidding on oily parking lots or slipping off yellow domes, those blister bumps on crosswalks. I learned a lot about priorities, patience, acceptance and appreciation. Accepting my limitations prompted patience with my own, as well as others' frailties.

Tom: When Joan got hurt and our roles flipped, it was time to step up. Cooking, helping and caring were needed, but my first priority was learning. My crash course in Joan 101 also involved laundry and plant care. I just had to be careful to keep all their foods separate. Orchids don't like spaghetti. But apparently our camellias liked coffee. My final exam was doing it all myself. I became a better husband. Who knew there was room!

Joan: Sitting in Los Angeles traffic with appointment deadlines looming used to trouble me. Strict elementary school discipline overlaid with threats and punishment had taught my anxious child-self to believe that lateness for any reason was inexcusable. It's certainly not desirable, but it may be pardonable. When I'm unavoidably delayed now, I see it as an opportunity to do foot flexions and extensions or Kegel exercises. I now view the world and the diversity of people in it, including myself, with more tolerance.

Tom: My wife's changes have made it harder for me to be idle. Joan now tries to make every spare moment productive. While we're in the car waiting for a light to change, she does Kegel exercises. Are others nearby also working muscles that support their bladder, small intestine and rectum? It makes me uneasy. Should I be Kegeling for my prostate? For those like Joan and me who don't sing well, maybe Carpool Kegeling will be the next big thing.

CHAPTER THIRTY-FOUR

One More Step

Joan: I had been cooped up for almost two years. I was discharged by my surgeon three months after the second surgery. X-rays looked good. I started walking around the neighborhood without pain, but without the sense of wonder and discovery of walking in a forest. I told Tom I needed to finish the hike that we started at Rose Valley Falls. I wondered whether my foot could handle what it used to. I was anxious about it, but had to face it.

Tom: That's exactly what I was waiting to hear, but I didn't suggest it. I wanted that to come from Joan. I made plans before she could change her mind. The next day after a trip to the market, I loaded my backpack with our favorite lunches along with the rest of my gear.

I was eager to get back to the forest too. I grew up a city boy in Philadelphia without even one tree on my street of row houses. How sad for the dogs too! I got my first real taste of nature after I met Joan. Her house was next to a forest-like park. That's where her love of the outdoors began. The park had steep hills for sledding, a frozen pond for ice skating, and a tennis court—oddly without fences. Retrieving balls was quicker if you brought your dog.

Joan: Except for my dog, that is. Benny was an older dachshund. He would run after a ball, then get tired. We had to run after him, and carry him and the ball back.

Tom: I'm glad she didn't have an old St. Bernard. The park was where Joan found her first patients—injured squirrels, rabbits and birds that she nursed back to health without co-pays.

Joan: We arrived at the Rose Valley Falls trailhead. Getting out of our car, I heard something familiar—*Tchur-tchur,* the call of a woodpecker. Then came the Morse Code-like response of another woodpecker drumming. I've always wondered why, with all that head-banging, a woodpecker doesn't get a concussion.

Tom: I googled it. Unlike in football, something huge doesn't come crashing into the bird! That little pecker is the aggressor. The woodpecker has a unique bone in its head that acts like a seatbelt for its brain.

A human brain floats freely. A strong impact sends it ricocheting off the inside of the skull, causing a concussion. A football helmet protects only the outside of the head. Maybe someday players' brains will be protected with a medical version of packing noodles. Glassware and electronics packed in noodles arrived at our house intact. It didn't matter how far the delivery guy tossed them.

Joan: The Rose Valley Falls Trail looked different. The year before, a huge wildfire had swept through the area and cleared the chaparral. The Forest Service had done an impressive job of removing dead trees and debris that remained. Not only did their work make the trail passable, it also allowed grasses, wildflowers and shrubs to sprout and begin healing the forest.

Tom: Signs of life were visible everywhere, especially in leafy new branches emerging from apparently dead trees. The character and tenacity of the remaining charred trees stood in contrast to the youthful glow of their new neighbors below.

On our hikes Joan enjoyed nature's oddities, like how hummingbirds could fly backwards. Joan pointed to one doing it right off the trail. Kinda made sense. Hummingbirds were always poking their heads into flowers and many had bees in them. They had to slam it in reverse and back their butts outta there!

Joan: Hummingbirds and bees aren't enemies. Together they function as a garden's dating service. They land on pollen from the male part of a flower and deposit it on the female part of another flower. Eventually love blooms, even though the two flowers didn't even meet for coffee.

Joan: As we walked, we started to gain elevation. There weren't steps and a handrail like at Physical Therapy, but I was okay with it. Climbing was no problem. I was glad that my muscles felt strong again. Farther along we approached a stream. I remembered how slippery those moss-covered rocks were, but this time I was wearing waterproof hiking boots.

Tom: I remembered that after Joan's injury, her balance had been affected. I offered to sell Joan my hiking stick. She thanked me, but said she had left her loose change in the car. She thought I should keep it because I had already slipped into the water once. Most of all, she wanted to see if she could handle crossing the stream like she did before her accident.

Joan: Some of the rocks were high and dry. Others tilted into the water at strange angles, and were too far apart for an easy leap. Some rocked like cradles and so did I. Wobbling here and there, I almost spilled my wine. Just kidding! I had to make a few mid-stream course corrections onto some flat-top rocks. After a couple short hops, I made it to the other side without losing my footing or slipping into the water. It felt great! I started to leave my doubts behind.

Tom: Joan looked happy. I could see her confidence growing. While I was waiting for her, I noticed some mushrooms growing. I kept it to myself.

Joan: I got jazzed when I spotted umbrella-shaped mushrooms huddled at the base of a tree. How about that! They came back after the fire. I asked Tom whether I had told him about how these particular mushrooms influenced architecture.

Tom: I said I remembered something about mushrooms and marriage licenses, and the law wasn't on my side.

Uh-oh, I sensed class was about to start!

Joan: Tom said he'd *love* to hear more. I shared how the mushroom structure became the blueprint for buildings. Frank Lloyd Wright's mushroom house is famous. So are Earl Young's delightful Hobbit houses with their curved windows and roofs. It was another example of how the man-made world often echoes the natural one. Then to check if Tom was listening, I added something about how an observant architect, walking in a shady grove, was inspired after seeing impish elves living in colorful mushroom houses nearby.

Tom: I smiled and said I'd try not to step on them.

Joan: The distant sound of the waterfall made me pick up the pace. Our efforts were rewarded when we spotted a bench-like rock with a view of the falls. We were wowed again by the power and constancy of it. Yet off to the sides, delicate rivulets sparkled like shiny ribbons in the sunlight, while thin sheets of water glided gently down the steep wall of sandstone.

Tom: I unpacked our favorite lunches. For Joan, it was chicken curry with apples and raisins. For me it was chicken diablo—pasta, peppers and white meat in heat!

Joan: We savored every bite while enjoying the cooling mist. The falls were loud and powerful, but strangely peaceful at the same time.

I was grateful that my foot didn't hurt, and I was able to revisit this place.

Tom took a bag from his backpack to pick up some trash. He said he had noticed some soda cans and candy wrappers tossed near a boulder behind us. As he left to get them, I was a bit disappointed. Tom didn't pull out a surprise dessert like he had in the past. While he was gone, I peeked into his backpack. Nothing there.

Tom: I came back and started putting our take-out containers into my trash bag. I told Joan I forgot to get some trash back there that was up on a ledge. I asked her to grab it while I packed up our things. She walked back around the boulder.

Joan: Calling to Tom, I said it was too high. I looked up again, and noticed it was a pink box ... tied with ... white string ... so it didn't look empty.

Tom: I came around and told her she didn't need me. She could reach it. What was all that surgery and physical therapy for?

Joan: Raising my arm, I showed him it was way over my head.

Tom: I told Joan she was probably right. We should get our stuff and head home.

Joan: Wait, something was up, I thought! That pink box made me curious.

To strengthen my foot enough to reach the top shelves at home, I had been doing heel and toe lifts. That pink box gave me extra motivation. I got high up on my toes and stretched to my limit. For the longest time, I hadn't done that.

My fingernail barely hooked the string so I could pull the box down. As it got close, it smelled really good. Tom grinned. I teasingly asked him to cut the string with his Swiss Army Knife. His grin disappeared. Moments later, a triumphant smile crossed his face. He smugly removed his credit card size multi-tool from his wallet, and sliced the string.

Tom: I told Joan she had worked hard to get better, and we should celebrate.

Joan: He was right. For the first time in almost two years, I was sure I was back on my game.

I lifted the lid. When I finally stopped laughing, I gave Tom a kiss. In the box, on top of a small cheesecake majestically stood two chocolate crutches tipped with banana peels.

Tom: "Since you're all better, don't you think it would be a nice gesture to donate those crutches to charity like you said people should do?" She ate them before she answered.

Joan: Tom used my weakness to make me feel strong. I finally had sweet memories of crutches and Rose Valley Falls. It was a fantastic day with Tom who helped me do what I loved again.

CHAPTER THIRTY-FIVE

Appendix A:

Assemble Before Surgery

Prepare the bed and bedside:

—Clean bed linens

Leave untucked the bottom of the sheet and blanket to allow space for a very large cast, but not as large as the cast of *Hamilton.*

—A slant pillow with platform to elevate your legs and feet above your heart

—Extra blankets and pillows

—Medical device: Multi-purpose Cold Therapy/DVT Compression Unit

—A bedside table, plus extension cord if needed

—Thermometer to monitor any post-surgical infection

—Daily medications and vitamins to be joined by post-op meds

—Pitcher or bottles of water, cups, small packaged snacks

—Echo Dot (Alexa) for reminders, or a timer

(You can also dump your frustrations on Alexa,
and she won't yell back.)

—Bicycle horn to get Tom's attention if he's in
another room

—Whistle to tell him "Never mind!"

—Eyeglasses to misplace and find several times a
day

—Breathable eye mask to block nighttime lights
from electronics and blinking medical devices

—Flashlight to search for things that dropped

—Tissues, nail files, moist towelettes

—A few small towels as placemats for meals in
bed (Invite your dog up to get rid of crumbs.)

—Trash basket

—Wallet and credit cards for online orders and
rentals

—Pepper spray if you're alone, or for a visitor
who complains her pain is worse than yours

—Knee Scooter

—Clock

—Skateboard—just kidding!

—Recliner or foot stool to elevate your foot once
you're out of bed

—No-skid sock or slipper—just one for the good
foot, but don't expect a store discount

—Later I used a rectangular plastic container to ice
my foot in. Tom filled it, and occasionally
dropped in a few rubber frogs and fish.

Closet:

—Longer skirts or pants that I could pull over the cast,
    like zip-off hiking pants, or wide-leg shorts
    in summer

—A vest, shirt or apron with pockets to carry a phone
    etc.

Bathroom near the den:

—Use a non-skid mat for the shower and/or tub
    Picture several firefighters and paramedics
    stomping in to haul naked you out of your
    contorted position on the floor of the tub
    or shower.

—Towels and washcloths

—Pajamas

—Stack of underwear, socks, slippers

—Lotions, moisturizer, make-up

—Toothpaste, brushes, floss

—Deodorant

—Hair blower, hair care products, brushes, combs

—Shower cap

—Tampons

—Razor or electric shaver (Not to be used on the
    cat when you're bored)

—Soap, shampoo and conditioner

—Plastic Leg Sleeve to keep cast dry in the tub
    or shower

—Hamper

CHAPTER THIRTY-SIX

Appendix B:

Insurance as a Second Language

Tom: There are basically two different types of health insurance —managed care and indemnity plans. With managed care, patients see a network of medical providers chosen by their insurer, which helps to contain costs. With an indemnity plan, patients may go to whichever doctors they choose, then pay what insurance doesn't. The freedom of choice tends to cost more. Our insurance is an indemnity plan.

A while back, I received an insurance statement for the facility where Joan had one of her foot surgeries done. In a box labeled "Billed," there was a charge of $10,953. In the next box labeled "Discount," $9,762 was listed. "Wow, the Surgery Center must have had a big sale on feet! Were we lucky!" I thought.

Actually our insurance plan got the discount. It paid only the $1,191 difference, per their agreement of allowable charges for Surgery Centers. We benefited too. Our obligation under that agreement was only $242. Because Joan had gotten a referral for surgery at an in-network facility, that charge was reduced further. It paid to know the options that our health insurance plan provided.

Insurance statements can be confusing in other ways, I learned, while dealing with all of Joan's medical bills. One came with the name of a doctor we had never heard of, stating that we owed him money for "Medical Care." Who was this mystery man, I wondered, who wanted to be paid for nothing in particular?

Fortunately the Claims department of our plan could answer my question. All charges and reimbursements flowed through them. They revealed that the phantom doctor had read one of Joan's EKGs. He must have been a speed-reader 'cause we owed him only $1.84!

Just as charges can be puzzling, so can insurance policies with vague clauses about what they'll cover—like "subject to the limitations noted earlier," anything that starts with "in lieu of" and "not withstanding" plus a personal favorite, "without limiting the generality of the foregoing." At least there's one clause you never have to fear— Santa Claus. But even he doesn't give you everything you want. Neither does every insurance plan.

Joan: We're grateful every day for the Writers' Guild-Industry Health Fund, which is now our secondary insurance since Medicare became primary. They still administer our claims. It's not their fault I leaped off that boulder. In fact they had every right to mutter some snarky remarks which they did not. Fortunately those who worked there answered the phone and were friendly. People contacting some insurance companies have reported preparing several course meals while waiting on speaker because of the biggest lie ever told, "Your call is very important to us."

Tom: Over the years, Joan and I have discussed many kinds of claims with many Claims representatives. We've learned the good and less effective ways of doing it, and that's what I'd like to share. Issues were eventually sorted out, often to our liking but not always. If a procedure wasn't covered, we were told why. I remember when one rep actually read a part of our policy to me over the phone so I would understand the denial. It was the first time a woman had read to me since my mother, though I liked the ending of my mom's stories better.

Before that, I regarded reading insurance policies as a treatment for insomnia. Afterwards I realized that I could understand them if I took the time to study what was in them.

Years ago, I caused a few claims discussions to escalate more than they had to, but the Claims reps kept their cool, and I learned from them. They weren't Stormtroopers, and I didn't have to be a Jedi Knight. They were normal people with families, just like us. Yes, they were allowed to breed too. Good manners were appreciated, since they were often yelled at by other callers. We spoke to them the same way we wanted to be spoken to.

If you're stonewalled by a Claims rep, KEEP YOUR COOL, while calmly stating your case. Your job is two-fold. First, know the key provisions of the insurance you have. Second, be persistent, but polite if you think you're right. If you make the Claims department your enemy, you're sabotaging yourself.

The good news is that insurance claims that had been denied can be appealed. Only facts, not emotion, should be included during claims discussions. You don't need to reenact your symptoms to show how sick you were. They don't want to feel your pain.

During an appeal, the insurance company often will request more information to support why your treatment was necessary. Get it in writing from your doctor, then pay a pharmacist to translate his scribbles.

Joan: A key question always is "Was your claim submitted properly?" Be sure that the correct billing code was entered by the doctor's staff because one wrong letter or number could result in denial.

For my first foot surgery, if Dr. Five Potato had entered an incorrect code, my mistakenly submitted "prostate removal" would not be covered, and neither would my foot surgery. Writing this book, I corrected lots of my own typos, so I *no* how *weasily* that can *happan*.

Tom: Happily no appeals were needed for either of Joan's foot surgeries. There was one insurance statement, though, that had to be reprocessed. It was from a surgical facility which showed that we owed more than we did—$1700 more! For whatever reason, our referral number for surgery in a network facility never made it from the facility to Claims, who unknowingly processed the claim incorrectly.

I knew the charge was wrong from being aware of our coverages, especially how a specific kind of referral can reduce charges. However, it took me more time than I thought to dig out the information that Claims should have already been sent.

I would rather have spent that time in the kitchen. Joan really liked mashed avocados on toast for lunch. I had been practicing how to cut avocados in half and remove the stone without chunks of my finger. Mashed avocados on toast should be a vegetarian dish.

Joan: The best insurance advice we ever got was to become familiar with our policy. It will help you rest easier when insurance statements arrive. It saved us money on our medical care, and it could save you money too.

Acknowledgments

Joan: Thank you, Tom, for putting your life on hold to care for me. At times I was scared, but you were encouraging and positive. Mornings began with a big smile and a hug, followed by the mug of hot coffee you handed me—for only a dollar. "Don't worry about it now," you said, "I bill at the end of the month." Then you brought me breakfast in bed, along with a basin of hot soapy water so I could wash my dishes. You did that once and broke me up. I love and appreciate you.

You made me laugh when our situation wasn't funny. Pantomiming with glow sticks and orange batons, you were ahead in the hallway, marshaling me on my knee scooter as if it were a taxiing airplane—even though your randomly swinging arms would have guided me into a wall! I could have found the bathroom without you, but you really seemed to be having a good time.

Outside as we walked side by side, either I would accidentally trip you with my renegade crutch, or you, wanting to stay helpfully close, were inadvertently tripping me. We needed a choreographer as well as a doctor. My injury was unintended, but the experience turned into something rewarding by bringing us closer together.

Being able to co-write this book with you, a professional TV writer, was a big step up the creative ladder for me. I felt weightless and carefree being with you on that ladder, not deterred by my disabled foot. My spirits were lifted as we wrote and laughed together.

Our ping-ponging points of view scored some good work. Your perspective often came from a place where no compass points. Amazing thoughts developed in that savvy silver spot somewhere in your grey matter. One-of-a-kind notions found their way out of the twisting noodles of your brain. Keep on noodling.

❀　　❀　　❀

Also thanks to friends and family who cared for and visited me. You brought joy and diversion to my housebound routine. I'm grateful for your help in breaking the cycle of convalescence and loneliness. I'll carry your kindnesses with me.

Thank you to the good doctors and their staffs, and the physical therapists who made my return to active life possible.

❀　　❀　　❀

Tom: I want to thank the boulder that Joan jumped off of for making this book possible. Feel proud, boulder, you now have a literary cachet.

I also want to commend you, Joan, for trusting a caregiver who could make you laugh, but not do much else at first without your help. It was a good tip not to toast bread with jelly already on it.

Joan, early in our marriage you were the main breadwinner until I got jobs writing for comedians, then TV shows. You always believed in my writing, and that kept me at it. Asking me to write this book with you, however, was a surprise. You reminded me that we experienced everything together. We just had different roles. As we wrote, we relived upsetting, confusing and amusing moments. Collaborating was fun and cathartic, and it let me discover what an intelligent, sensitive and humorous writer you are. Your narrative was precise and fluid, your descriptions often poetic. I'm glad to be your partner in yet another way.

Sorry, boulder, but I just have more to thank Joan for than you. Please don't roll down from the forest and crush my car.

✿ ✿ ✿

Joan and Tom: We are both grateful to author, Linda Peters. Linda, your keen eye for detail and clarity of thinking improved our storytelling. Your notes were specific and at times inspired, making our revisions enjoyable.

We also appreciate your guidance through the many steps of the publishing process, including your recommendation for our cover designer. This project would have been far more challenging without your help. Thank you, Linda, for leading the way.

To Our Readers

Thank you for being interested enough to pick up our book and spend your valuable time reading it. We hope we shared useful information while making you laugh. Your part of our reader/writer relationship kept us motivated. We'll be writing more books, and we look forward to connecting with you again.

If you enjoyed our book, please consider leaving a review. A good review will help us as well as others looking for their next good read.

Connect with us on our Facebook Page:
Humor Hill Publishing

Or email at:
HumorHillPublishing@gmail.com

❀ ❀ ❀

In memory of Liz

❀ ❀ ❀

Made in the USA
Columbia, SC
10 November 2020

24250832R00107